MW00813813

Fish and Game Laws of Massachusetts

FISH AND GAME
LAWS

MASSACHUSETTS
1908

Commissioners

GEORGE W. FIELD   JOHN W. DELANO

GEORGE H. GARFIELD

Fish and Game Laws

OF

MASSACHUSETTS.

PUBLISHED BY THE

Commissioners on Fisheries and Game.

COMMISSIONERS:

GEORGE W. FIELD, CHAIRMAN,
JOHN W. DELANO, SUPT. OF HATCHERIES,
GEORGE H GARFIELD.

Office, Room 158, State House, Boston.

BOSTON:
WRIGHT & POTTER PRINTING CO., STATE PRINTERS,
18 POST OFFICE SQUARE.
1908.

APPROVED BY
THE STATE BOARD OF PUBLICATION.

CONTENTS.

FISH LAWS.

CONTENTS.

FISH AND GAME LAWS

OF

MASSACHUSETTS,

1908.

FISH — WHEN NOT TO BE TAKEN.

	PENALTIES.
Pike Perch not to be in possession or transported between Feb. 1 and June 1 .	$50
Black Bass under 8 inches in length not to be taken . .	$10
Pickerel, under 10 inches in length not to be taken . .	$1
Trout, Lake Trout and Landlocked Salmon close season is between Aug. 1 and April 15 in all counties . . .	$10 to $25
Trout less than 6 inches in length not to be taken . .	$10
Wild Trout not to be bought, sold or offered for sale . for each fish	$1
Salmon . . . . . between Aug. 1 and May 1	$10 to $50
Smelt . . . . between March 15 and June 1	$1
Lobsters, alive, not to be less than 9 inches in length; boiled, not to be less than 8¾ inches in length . .	$5
Lobsters, not to be mutilated . . .	$5
Lobsters bearing Eggs . . not to be taken at any season	$10 to $100
Nets and Trawls . . not to be used in ponds under penalty of	$20 to $50
Not exceeding ten hcoks to be used in ponds under penalty of	$20 to $50
Explosives and Poisons not to be used in fishing waters . .	$10

.

FISH LAWS.

AUTHORITY OF COMMISSIONERS ON FISHERIES AND GAME, ETC.

What constitute fisheries laws.

SECTION 1. All laws relative to the culture, preservation, capture or passage of fish shall be known as the laws relative to fisheries.

Appointment of fish and game commissioners.

SECTION 2. There shall be a board of commissioners on fisheries and game consisting of three persons who shall be appointed by the governor, with the advice and consent of the council, for the term of five years from the time of their appointments and who shall be removable at the pleasure of the governor.

As AMENDED BY ACTS OF 1905, CHAP. 407.

Authority to remove obstructions to migratory fish.

SECTION 3. The commissioners are empowered to appoint deputies, and each of the commissioners, the deputies of the commissioners or members of the district police may enforce the laws regulating fisheries; and may seize and remove, summarily if need be, all illegal obstructions to the passage of migratory fish except dams, mills or machinery, at the expense of the persons using or maintaining the same.

ACTS OF 1908, CHAP. 417.

Authority of the commissioners and their deputies to enforce laws.

SECTION 1. The commissioners on fisheries and game and their salaried deputies shall have and exercise throughout the commonwealth for the enforcement of the laws relating to fish,

birds and mammals, all the powers of constables,
except the service of civil process, and of police-
men and watchmen.   The said salaried deputies
when on duty shall wear, and shall display as a
token of authority, a metallic badge bearing the
seal of the commonwealth and the words "Deputy Fish and Game Commissioner."

SECTION 2.   Any person not being a salaried
deputy of said commission on fisheries and game
who shall possess or wear the above described
badge shall be punished by a fine of ten dollars
for every such offence.

SECTION 3.   The commissioners on fisheries and
game, with the approval of the governor, may in
writing authorize any of their salaried deputies
to have in possession and carry a revolver, club,
billy, handcuffs and twisters, or such other
weapon or article as may be required in the performance of their official duty.

ACTS OF 1908, CHAP. 255.

May require display for inspection.

A commissioner on fisheries and game or any
duly authorized deputy commissioner, receiving
a salary from the commonwealth, may request
of any person whom said commissioner or deputy
commissioner reasonably believes to be engaged
in the taking, killing, hunting or snaring of fish,
birds or animals, contrary to law, that such person shall forthwith display for the inspection of
such commissioner or deputy commissioner, any
and all fish, birds and animals then in his possession; and upon refusal to comply with such
request said commissioner or duly authorized
deputy commissioner may arrest without warrant
the person so refusing.

Can arrest without warrant.

SECTION 4.   The commissioners and their
deputies, members of the district police and all
officers qualified to serve criminal process may

arrest without warrant any person whom they find violating any of the fish or game laws, except that persons engaged in the business of regularly dealing in the buying and selling of game as an article of commerce shall not be so arrested for having in possession or selling game at their usual places of business.

ACTS OF 1907, CHAP. 299.

Duties with respect to forest and other fires.

The commissioners on fisheries and game and their duly authorized deputies may arrest without a warrant any person found in the act of unlawfully setting a fire. Said commissioners and their deputies may require assistance according to the provisions of section twenty of chapter thirty-two of the Revised Laws, and they shall take precautions to prevent the progress of forest fires, or the improper kindling thereof, and upon the discovery of any such fire shall immediately summon the necessary assistance, and notify the forest fireward of the town.

ACTS OF 1904, CHAP. 367.

The right of search.

SECTION 1.   Any commissioner on fisheries and game, deputy commissioner on fisheries and game, member of the district police, or officer qualified to serve criminal process, may, with a warrant, search any boat, car, box, locker, crate or package, and any building, where he has reason to believe any game or fish taken or held in violation of law is to be found, and may seize any game or fish so taken or held, and any game or fish so taken or held shall be forfeited: *provided, however,* that this section shall not authorize entering a dwelling house, or apply to game or fish which is passing through this Commonwealth under authority of the laws of the United States.

SECTION 2.   A court or justice authorized to issue warrants in criminal cases shall, upon complaint under oath that the complainant believes that any game or fish unlawfully taken or held is concealed in a particular place, other than a dwelling house, if satisfied that there is reasonable cause for such belief, issue a warrant to search therefor. The search warrant shall designate and describe the place to be searched and the articles for which search is to be made, and shall be directed to any officer named in section one of this act, commanding him to search the place where the game or fish for which he is required to search is believed to be concealed, and to seize such game or fish.

To regulate brook fishing.

SECTION 5. If the owner of land within which a brook is wholly or partly situated agrees that such brook or part thereof shall be open to the public after the expiration of three years as hereinafter provided, the commissioners may, upon petition of thirty or more inhabitants of a city or town within which such brook is wholly or partly situated, including such owner, or upon petition of the mayor and aldermen of such city or the selectmen of such town and such owner, cause such brook to be stocked with food fish; and shall then make reasonable regulations, which shall be in force for a period of not more than three years, relative to fishing in such brook, may affix penalties of not more than twenty dollars for each violation thereof and shall cause such regulations to be enforced. There shall be allowed and paid annually from the treasury of the commonwealth an amount not exceeding five hundred dollars to carry out the provisions of this section.

Commissioners' authority to take fish.

SECTION 6. The commissioners may take fish or cause them to be taken at any time or in any manner for purposes connected with fish culture or scientific observation.

As amended by Acts of 1902, Chap. 164.

Fishing permits.

SECTION 7. The board of commissioners on fisheries and game may issue permits for the taking of sand eels in the tidal waters of the Merrimac and Ipswich rivers and Plum Island sound, and their tributaries. Said permits shall be issued without any fee therefor, and shall be revocable at the discretion of the commissioners.

ACTS OF 1902, CHAP. 178.

Investigations.

The authority of the commissioners on fisheries and game shall extend to the investigation of questions relating to fish and fisheries, or to game, and they may from time to time, personally or by assistants, institute and conduct inquiries pertaining to such questions.

ACTS OF 1906, CHAP. 327.

The protection of property and material used by the commissioners on fisheries and game in making scientific investigations.

Whoever wilfully and without right enters in or upon any building or other structure or any area of land or water set apart and used by or under authority of the commissioners on fisheries and game for conducting scientific experiments or investigations after said commissioners have caused printed notices of such occupation and use and the purposes thereof to be placed in a conspicuous position adjacent to any such areas of land or water or upon any such building or other structure, and any person who wilfully and maliciously injures or defaces any such building or other structure or any notice posted as aforesaid, or injures or destroys any property used in such experiments or investigations, or otherwise interferes therewith, shall be punished by imprisonment for not more than six months or by a fine of not more than two hundred dollars. And said commissioners and their deputies are hereby authorized to arrest without warrant any person found violating the provisions of this act.

Section 8, Revised Laws, as amended by Acts of 1906,
Chap. 356.

Sawdust pollution.

SECTION 1. If the commissioners determine that the fish of any brook or stream in this commonwealth are of sufficient value to warrant the prohibition or regulation of the discharge therein of sawdust from sawmills, and that the discharge of sawdust from any particular sawmill materially injures such fish, they may, by an order in writing to the owner or tenant of such sawmill, prohibit or regulate the discharge of sawdust therefrom into such brook or stream. Such order may be revoked or modified by them at any time. Before any such order is made said commissioners shall, after reasonable notice to all parties in interest, give a public hearing in the county where the sawmill to be affected by the order is located, at which hearing any citizen shall have the right to be heard on the questions to be determined by the commissioners. Upon petition of any party aggrieved by such order, filed within six months after the date thereof, the superior court, sitting in equity, may, after such notice as it may deem sufficient, hear all interested parties and annul, alter or affirm said order. Whoever, having been so notified, discharges sawdust or suffers or permits it to be discharged from a sawmill under his control into a brook or stream in violation of the order of said commissioners, or of said court, if an appeal is taken, shall be punished by a fine of not more than twenty-five dollars.

SECTION 2. Any person aggrieved by an order made by the commissioners on fisheries and game relative to the discharge of sawdust into streams, under the provisions of section eight of said chapter ninety-one, and in force at the date of the passage of this act, shall be entitled, upon application to the commissioners on fisheries and game, to a public hearing and petition to the superior court, as provided in section one hereof.

SECTION 3. This act shall take effect upon its passage.

AS AMENDED BY ACTS OF 1904, CHAP. 365.

FISHWAYS.

Authority of commissioners to examine, etc.

SECTION 9. The commissioners may examine all dams upon rivers where the law requires fishways to be maintained, or where in their judgment fishways are needed, and they shall determine whether the fishways, if any, are suitable and sufficient for the passage of the fish in such rivers, or whether in their judgment a fishway is needed for the passage of fish over any dam; and shall prescribe by an order in writing what changes or repairs, if any, shall be made therein, and where, how and when a new fishway must be built, and at what times the same shall be kept open, and shall give notice to the owners of the dams accordingly. The supreme judicial court, or the superior court, shall, upon the petition of the commissioners, have jurisdiction in equity or otherwise to enforce any order made in accordance with the provisions of this section, and to restrain any violation of such order.

Notification of dam owners.

SECTION 10. Such owners shall be notified by serving upon them a copy of the order; and a certificate of the commissioners that service has been so made shall be deemed sufficient proof thereof.

Liability of owners.

SECTION 11. Any owner of such a dam who refuses or neglects to keep open or maintain a fishway at the times prescribed by the commissioners shall forfeit fifty dollars for each day of such refusal or neglect.

Commissioners can build, etc.

SECTION 12. If, in the opinion of the commissioners, a passage for edible fish should be provided, or if any one of the commissioners finds that there is no fishway or an insufficient fishway in or around a dam where a fishway is required by law to be maintained, any one of the commissioners may, in his discretion, enter with workmen and materials upon the premises of the person required to maintain a fishway there and may, at the expense of the commonwealth, if in the opinion of the commissioners the person required by law to construct or maintain such fishway is not able to afford such expense, improve an existing fishway, or cause one to be constructed if none exists, and may, if necessary, take the land of any other person who is not obliged by law to maintain said fishway; and if a fishway has been constructed in accordance with the provisions of this section, the commissioners shall not require the owner of the dam to alter such fishway within five years after the completion thereof.

Settlement of damages.

SECTION 13. All damages which are caused by taking land as provided in the preceding section, shall, upon the application of either party, be estimated in the same manner as land which has been taken for a highway and shall be paid by the commonwealth. Said expense shall be a charge against the person who is required by law to construct and maintain such fishway and shall be recovered in an action of contract in the name of the commonwealth, with costs and with interest at the rate of twelve per cent per annum.

Passage over private land.

SECTION 14. Each of the commissioners may, in the performance of his duties, enter upon and pass through or over private property.

ACTS OF 1902, CHAP. 138.

INSPECTION OF FISH.

Powers and duties of commissioners.

SECTION 1. The office of inspector general of fish is hereby abolished.

SECTION 2. The powers and duties heretofore conferred and imposed upon the inspector general of fish are hereby conferred and imposed upon the board of commissioners on fisheries and game.

SECTION 3. Said board may appoint in every town in which fish is packed for export, inspectors of fish, who shall be sworn before them or before a justice of the peace, and shall give bond to them with sufficient sureties, and be removable at the discretion of said board. Each inspector shall once in six months make the returns to said board necessary to carry into effect the provisions of chapter fifty-six of the Revised Laws.

SECTION 4. The inspectors of fish shall have the powers and perform the duties heretofore conferred and imposed upon the deputy inspectors of fish, but shall pay to the commissioners on fisheries and game the proportion of fees formerly paid to the inspector general of fish. Said commissioners shall pay the fees received from the inspectors into the treasury of the commonwealth on the first Monday of January and the first Monday of July in each year, and shall include a brief statement of the work of fish inspection and of the fees received therefor, in their annual report.

SECTION 5.   Sections three and four of chapter fifty-six of the Revised Laws are hereby repealed.

ACTS OF 1903, CHAP. 196.

Publication of returns of inspection of fish.

SECTION 1.   Section five of chapter fifty-six of the Revised Laws, which provides for an annual return and publication relative to the inspection of fish, is hereby repealed.

FISHERIES IN GREAT PONDS.

Public rights in great ponds.

SECTION 15.   The fishery of a pond, the area of which is more than twenty acres, shall be public, except as hereinafter provided; and all persons shall, for the purpose of fishing, be allowed reasonable means of access thereto.

Commissioners' control of ponds.

SECTION 16.   The commissioners may occupy, manage and control not more than six great ponds, except such as have revested in the commonwealth for breach of the terms and conditions of any lease thereof, for the purpose of cultivating useful fish and of distributing them within the commonwealth; and may occupy not more than one-tenth part thereof with enclosures and appliances for the purpose of such cultivation; but this privilege shall not affect any public rights to such ponds, other than the right of fishing, and the appliances and enclosures shall be so placed as not to debar ingress to or egress from such ponds at proper places.

SECTION 17.   If the commissioners determine so to occupy and improve any such pond, they shall post a notice of such purpose in a public place in the town or towns in which said pond is situated and file a like notice in the office of the

clerk of each of said towns and in the office of the
secretary of the commonwealth. The affidavit
of an officer qualified to serve civil process that
such notice has been posted shall be deemed full
proof thereof.

SECTION 18. After such notice has been so
filed and posted, any violation of any of the
rights of said commissioners under the provisions of section sixteen shall be punished as
provided in section twenty-nine.

As AMENDED BY ACTS OF 1907, CHAP. 306.

Stocking great ponds with food fish.

SECTION 19. The commissioners, upon the
petition of the mayor and aldermen of a city or
of the selectmen of a town within which a great
pond or a portion thereof is situated, shall cause
the waters of such pond to be stocked with such
food fish as they judge to be best suited to such
waters. They shall thereupon prescribe, for a
period not exceeding three years, such reasonable regulations relative to the fishing in such
ponds and their tributaries, with such penalties,
not exceeding twenty dollars for one offence, as
they deem to be for the public interest, and shall
cause such regulations to be enforced. The
commissioners may restock a pond with fish and
extend the provisions of this section for an
additional period of three years whenever they
receive a petition therefor as herein provided.
Five hundred dollars shall be annually appropriated by the Commonwealth to carry out the
provisions of this section.

Mill pond, Yarmouth.

SECTION 20. The commissioners may occupy
and control Mill pond, in the town of Yarmouth,
for the purpose of cultivating food fish for distribution within the commonwealth. Whoever,
without the written consent of the commissioners, fishes in said pond in any other manner

than with hand line and single hook, shall forfeit
not less than fifty nor more than two hundred
dollars for the first offence, and not less than one
hundred nor more than two hundred dollars for
any subsequent offence.

Measurement of ponds.

SECTION 21. The county commissioners shall,
in July, upon the request and at the expense of
any persons who claim to be interested in a great
pond, cause a measurement thereof to be made
which shall be recorded in the office of the town
clerk of each town within which such pond is
situated; and no arm or branch shall be included
as a part of a pond unless it is at least fifty feet
in width and one foot in depth.

SECTION 22. The selectmen of a town may
measure ponds which are wholly within their
town, in the manner provided in the preceding
section, and such measurement shall be recorded
in the office of the town clerk.

Private ownership of ponds.

SECTION 23. The riparian proprietors of any
pond, the area of which is not more than twenty
acres, and the proprietors of any pond or parts
of a pond created by artificial flowing shall have
exclusive control of the fisheries therein.

**Private ownership of ponds bounded in part by
public lands.**

SECTION 24. A pond which is not more than
twenty acres in area and is bounded in part by
land belonging to a town or county shall become
the exclusive property of the individual proprietors as to the fisheries therein only upon
payment to the town treasurer, county commissioners or treasurer and receiver general of a just
compensation for their respective rights therein,
to be determined by three persons, one of whom
shall be a riparian proprietor of said pond, one
the chairman of the board of selectmen, if the

rights of a town are in question, or of the county commissioners, if the rights of a county or of the commonwealth are in question, and one to be appointed by the commissioners on fisheries and game.

SECTION 25. Whoever, without the written consent of the proprietor or lessee of a natural pond, the area of which is not more than twenty acres, or of an artificial pond of any size, in which fish are lawfully cultivated and maintained, takes any fish therefrom, shall forfeit not more than twenty-five dollars for each offence.

As AMENDED BY ACTS OF 1904, CHAP. 308.

Prohibited apparatus for pond fishing.

SECTION 26. Whoever draws, sets, stretches or uses a drag net, set net, purse net, seine or trawl, or whoever sets or uses more than ten hooks for fishing, in any pond, or aids in so doing, shall be punished by a fine of not less than twenty nor more than fifty dollars. The provisions of this section shall not affect the rights of riparian proprietors of ponds mentioned in section twenty-three or the corporate rights of any fishing company.

CONTROL OF FISHERIES BY RIPARIAN PROPRIETORS.

For cultivation of fish.

SECTION 27. A riparian proprietor of an unnavigable stream may, within the limits of his own premises, enclose the waters thereof for the cultivation of useful fish *if he furnishes a suitable passage for migratory fish naturally frequenting such waters.*

When fish are private property.

SECTION 28. Fish which are artificially propagated or maintained shall be the property of the person propagating or maintaining them. A person who is legally engaged in their culture and maintenance may take them in his own waters at pleasure, and may have them in his possession for purposes properly connected with said culture and maintenance, and may at all times sell them for these purposes, but shall not sell them for food at seasons when their capture is prohibited by law.

Penalty for unauthorized fishing.

SECTION 29. Whoever, without the permission of the proprietors, fishes in that portion of a pond, stream or other water in which fish are lawfully cultivated or maintained shall forfeit not less than one nor more than twenty dollars for the first offence, and not less than five nor more than fifty dollars for any subsequent offence.

Definition of navigable stream.

SECTION 30. For the purposes of this chapter, no tidal stream shall be considered navigable above the point where, on the average throughout the year, it has a channel less than forty feet wide and four feet deep during the three hours nearest the hour of high tide.

Bounds can be fixed.

SECTION 31. The governor, with the advice and consent of the council, may, for the purposes of this chapter, arbitrarily fix and define the tidal bounds and mouths of streams upon the recommendation of the commissioners on fisheries and game.

Governor can limit fishing.

SECTION 32. The governor may, in like manner, limit or prohibit, for not more than five years at any one time, fishing in the navigable tidal waters and in the unnavigable waters of specified streams, except in such portions as may be enclosed according to provisions of section twenty-seven; and whoever fishes in streams where the right of fishing is thus limited or prohibited shall forfeit ten dollars for the first offence and fifty dollars for each subsequent offence.

Proprietors' rights.

SECTION 33. The riparian proprietor on an unnavigable tidal stream, enclosed or unenclosed, in which fish are lawfully cultivated or maintained shall have the control of the fishery thereof within his own premises and opposite thereto to the middle of the stream, and a riparian proprietor at the mouth of such stream, shall also have control of the fishing thereof beyond and around the mouth of the stream so far as the tide ebbs, if it does not ebb more than eighty rods; and whoever fishes within these limits without permission of such owner shall forfeit not less than one nor more than twenty dollars for the first offence and not less than five nor more than fifty dollars for each subsequent offence.

SHAD, HERRING AND ALEWIVES.

ACTS OF 1908, CHAP. 298.

The taking of herring in certain waters by means of torches or other light prohibited.

SECTION 1. It shall be unlawful for any person to display torches or other light designed or used for the purpose of taking herring in Hull bay, Quincy bay, Hingham harbor, or in any waters southerly of a line drawn from Moon Island to Pemberton.

SECTION 2. Whoever violates the provisions of this act shall, for a first offence, be punished by a fine of not less than fifty nor more than two hundred dollars or by imprisonment for not less than six nor more than twelve months, or by both such fine and imprisonment, and for a second offence, by both said fine and imprisonment.

Rights of towns and cities.

SECTION 34. A city or town may open ditches, sluiceways or canals into any pond within its limits for the introduction and propagation of herring or alewives, and for the creation of fisheries for the same; and land for opening such ditches, sluiceways or canals within such city or town may be taken according to the provisions of law for the taking of land for highways.

SECTION 35. A city or town which creates such fishery shall own it, may make regulations concerning it and may lease it for not more than five years, upon such terms as may be agreed upon. A town may lease for a like period, and upon like terms, any fishery owned by it or any public fishery regulated and controlled by it.

SECTION 36. Whoever takes, kills or hauls on shore any herring or alewives in a fishery created by a city or town, without its permission or that of its lessees, or in a fishery created by a corporation, without the permission of such corporation, shall forfeit not less than five nor more than fifty dollars. Prosecutions under the provisions of this section shall be commenced within thirty days after the commission of the offence.

Personal rights.

SECTION 37. The provisions of the three preceding sections shall not impair the rights of any person under any law passed before the twenty-fifth day of April in the year eighteen hundred and sixty-six or under any contract then existing, or authorize a city or town to enter upon or build canals or sluiceways into a pond which is the private property of a person or corporation.

ACTS OF 1904, CHAP. 321.

Relative to alewife fishery, Sandwich.

SECTION 1. Levi S. Nye and John A. Holway, their heirs and assigns, shall have for the term of ten years from the date of the passage of this

act, the exclusive right to take and catch alewives in the stream known as "Mill River", from
its sources in the "Shawme Lakes or Ponds", so-
called, through the marshes in the town of Sand-
wich to the waters of Cape Cod bay: *provided,*
that the said Nye and Holway, their heirs and
assigns, shall construct and maintain a good and
sufficient passageway over or around the dam
or dams which now are or may hereafter be
erected upon said stream to enable fish to enter
the ponds above such dam or dams, and shall
keep such passageway open and unobstructed
from the first day of April to the fourteenth day
of June, inclusive, of each year.

SECTION 2. Said Nye and Holway, and their
heirs and assigns, may catch alewives during two
thirds of the period specified in section one, that
is to say, upon fifty days out of the seventy-five
days between the first day of April and the fourteenth day of June, inclusive, of each year.

SECTION 3. Any person or persons taking alewives in said Mill river or in the said lakes or
ponds without the written consent of the said
Nye and Holway, or of their heirs and assigns,
shall, upon the complaint of said Nye or Holway,
or of their or any of their heirs or assigns, or of
any person in their behalf, forfeit not less than
ten nor more than twenty dollars for each offence.
Half of every such forfeiture shall be paid to said
Nye and Holway or to their heirs or assigns.

ACTS OF 1904, CHAP. 232.

Hummock pond, Nantucket.

SECTION 1. The inhabitants of the island of
Nantucket may take alewives or herring with
seines or nets in Hummock pond, south of the
bridge in the said island, from the tenth day of
March to the thirty-first day of May, inclusive,
in each year; but all fish, other than alewives or
herring, caught or taken in such seines or nets
shall immediately be put back in the water
whence they were taken.

SECTION 2. Any person violating the provisions of this act, by failing to put back immediately as aforesaid fish other than alewives or herring caught or taken as aforesaid, shall be punished by a fine of not less than twenty nor more than fifty dollars.

SECTION 3. So much of section twenty-six of chapter ninety-one of the Revised Laws as is inconsistent herewith is hereby repealed.

Fishing on Connecticut river.

SECTION 38. Whoever takes or aids in taking from the Connecticut river or its tributaries any shad or alewives between the first day of July and the fifteenth day of March shall forfeit one hundred dollars for each offence.

Fishing on Merrimac river.

SECTION 39. Whoever, from the first day of March to the thirty-first day of May, takes alewives above tidal waters in the Merrimac river or any tributary thereof between sunrise on Friday morning and sunrise on Monday morning shall, except as provided in section forty-one, forfeit for each alewife so taken not less than one nor more than five dollars.

SECTION 40. No person shall take shad in the Merrimac river in any manner between the first day of July and the first day of April.

Regulation of nets, etc.

SECTION 41. Whoever takes shad or alewives in that part of the Merrimac river where the tide ebbs and flows, by the use of a gill net of any description, or of a sweep seine having a mesh which stretches less than one and three-quarters inches, shall forfeit twenty-five dollars for each offence.

Methods and times of fishing.

SECTION 42. Whoever takes shad or alewives, except in the Connecticut, Taunton Great,

Nemasket and Merrimac rivers and their tributaries, in any other manner than by naturally or artificially baited hook and hand line, on Sunday, Tuesday or Thursday, and whoever, between the fifteenth day of June and the first day of March, takes shad, except in the Connecticut and Merrimac rivers, or alewives, shall forfeit for each shad five dollars, and for each alewife twenty-five cents.

Rights of lessees.

SECTION 43.   Lessees from the commissioners on fisheries and game of any body of water in the county of Dukes county and all other persons having the right to take alewives in any other waters in said county may at any time take alewives from said waters and from the ditches connecting them with each other and with the ocean. Whoever, other than said lessees or any other person duly authorized, takes any fish, except eels, from any of said waters or ditches without the previous permission in writing of said lessees or of said duly authorized person shall forfeit one dollar for each fish so taken.

ACTS OF 1904, CHAP. 132.

Authority of officers on Palmer's river.

SECTION 1.   The sheriff of the county of Bristol or any of his deputies, or any constable or fish warden of either of the towns of Swansea and Rehoboth, may without a warrant arrest any person whom he finds in the act of taking herring, alewives or shad from the waters of Palmer's river in either of said towns in violation of the provisions of chapter one hundred and thirty of the acts of the year eighteen hundred and thirty-six, or of chapter ninety-two of the acts of the year eighteen hundred and fifty-two, and may detain such person in a place of safe keeping until a warrant can be procured upon a complaint against him for said offence: *provided,* that the detention without a warrant shall not exceed twenty-four hours.

SECTION 2. Whoever violates the provisions of either of said chapters shall, in addition to the forfeitures therein provided, forfeit the seines or nets used in such unlawful taking of herring, alewives or shad.

REGULATION OF FISHING NEAR FISH-WAYS AND WITH NETS, ETC.

On Connecticut river.

SECTION 44. Whoever takes any fish within two hundred yards of any fishway on the Connecticut river or its tributaries, or trespasses within the limits of such fishway, shall forfeit fifty dollars for each offence. Whoever takes any fish beyond two hundred and within four hundred yards of any such fishway, in any other manner than by artificially or naturally baited hook and line, shall forfeit twenty-five dollars for each fish so taken.

On Merrimac river.

SECTION 45. Whoever takes any fish within four hundred yards of any fishway on the Merrimac river, or trespasses within the limits of such fishway, shall forfeit fifty dollars for each offence.

Net fishing season, Merrimac.

SECTION 46. Whoever, from the last day of May to the first day of March, uses a net of any description in the waters of the Merrimac river or any tributary thereof shall forfeit twenty-five dollars for each offence.

Gill net fishing prohibited.

SECTION 47. Whoever uses a gill net of any description in the waters of the Connecticut or Merrimac river or any tributary thereof shall forfeit twenty-five dollars for each offence.

Size of mesh.

SECTION 48.   Whoever, in taking herring or
mackerel, except with a dep net, in Mill river and
its tributaries in the city of Gloucester or the
towns of Essex and Ipswich, or in Plum Island
river and its tributaries in the towns of Ipswich,
Rowley or Newbury, uses a net or seine having a
mesh of less than one and three-quarters inches
shall be punished by a fine of twenty-five dollars
for each offence.

Size of seine mesh.

SECTION 49.   Whoever uses in the Connecticut,
Westfield, Deerfield, Miller's, Merrimac, Nashua
or Housatonic rivers, or any tributary thereof, a
sweep seine having a mesh which stretches less
than five inches shall forfeit twenty-five dollars
for the first offence, and fifty dollars for each subsequent offence.

When penalties do not apply.

SECTION 50.   The penalties prescribed by this
chapter for unlawful fishing in the Merrimac river
shall not apply to any person who draws a net or
seine with a mesh not less than two and one-
quarter inches after the twentieth day of June in
each year at any point in said river below the
Essex-Merrimac bridge, unless he takes salmon
or shad, nor if, while thus lawfully fishing, he
takes such fish and immediately returns it alive to
the waters from which it was taken.

Regulations on Connecticut river.

SECTION 51.   Whoever, between the fifteenth
day of March and the first day of July, sets or
uses, or aids in setting or using, in the Connecticut
river, a pound, weir or set net the meshes whereof
are less than two inches in extent, or between sunset on Saturday and sunrise on Monday sets or
draws, or aids in setting or drawing, a seine for
the purpose of taking fish in said river, and any

person owning or controlling in whole or in part a pound, weir or set net of any description, placed in said river, who, between sunset and sunrise as aforesaid, fails to keep the same open and free for the passage of fish in a manner satisfactory to the commissioners on fisheries and game shall forfeit four hundred dollars for each offence; and, in addition, shall forfeit such pounds, weirs and set nets.

Seining restrictions.

SECTION 52. Whoever uses a sweep seine or combination of sweep seines in such a manner as at any moment to close or seriously obstruct more than two-thirds of the width of a stream at the place where it is used, or delays or stops in paying out or hauling a sweep seine, or hauls a sweep seine within one-half mile of a point where such seine has been hauled within an hour, shall forfeit twenty-five dollars for the first offence, and fifty dollars for each subsequent offence; but the provisions of this section shall not apply to seines used in the smelt fisheries, or to the fisheries for shad or alewives in the Taunton Great river, or to the fisheries in North river in the county of Plymouth.

Restrictions, North river.

SECTION 53. Whoever sets a seine or combination of seines over three hundred and eighty-five feet in length, or casts a mesh net over three hundred and fifty feet in length, in the North river in the county of Plymouth shall for each offence be punished by a fine not less than twenty-five nor more than one hundred dollars or by imprisonment for not less than one nor more than three months.

Town and city fish wardens.

SECTION 54. The mayor and aldermen of cities and the selectmen of towns bordering on the Connecticut or Merrimac river shall appoint and

fix the compensation of one or more fish wardens
within their respective cities and towns, who
shall, respectively, make complaint of all offences
under the provisions of sections thirty-eight,
forty-four, forty-five and fifty-one.

Liability for neglect to appoint wardens.

SECTION 55. A city or town whose mayor and
aldermen or selectmen neglect to appoint and fix
the compensation of such fish wardens shall
forfeit not less than one hundred nor more than
five hundred dollars.

BLUEFISH.
In Wellfleet bay.

'SECTION 56. Whoever takes any bluefish in
the waters of Wellfleet bay in the town of Wellfleet with nets or seines, north and east of
Smalley's bar inside of a line drawn from Smalley's bar buoy east-southeast to the eastern
shore and west-northwest to the western shore,
shall forfeit one dollar for each bluefish so taken
or be punished by a fine of not more than one
hundred dollars.

SALMON AND TROUT.
Apparatus for salmon.

SECTION 57. Whoever takes a salmon, otherwise than with naturally or artificially baited
hook and hand line, shall be punished by a fine
of not less than fifty nor more than two hundred
dollars for each fish so taken; but a person who
so catches a salmon when lawfully fishing and
immediately returns it alive to the waters from
which it was taken shall not be subject to such
penalty.

Salmon season, etc.

SECTION 58. Whoever takes a salmon between
the first day of August and the first day of May,
and whoever at any time buys, sells or has in his

possession a salmon taken in this commonwealth between said dates, shall forfeit not less than ten nor more than fifty dollars for each offence; and whoever at any time buys, sells or has in his possession a young salmon less than one foot in length shall forfeit five dollars for every such salmon.

Salmon pots.

SECTION 59. Whoever at any time obstructs with a salmon pot more than one-half of a waterfall, channel or rapid or sets, uses, or maintains a salmon-pot the diameter of which is more than two feet, or who, when the taking of salmon is forbidden by law, sets, uses or maintains any salmon pot whatever, shall forfeit ten dollars for the first offence and twenty dollars for each subsequent offence.

Screens on the Merrimac.

SECTION 60. The commissioners on fisheries and game shall, during April, May and June, for the better protection of salmon fry in the Merrimac river, cause wire screens to be erected and maintained at the entrance of the canals in Lowell and Lawrence at the expense of the companies owning and operating said canals.

Liability for minors.

SECTION 61. If a minor takes a trout in any other manner than by hook and line in a town which accepts the provisions of this section or has accepted the corresponding provisions of earlier laws, his guardian shall forfeit one dollar for each trout so taken; but all prosecutions under the provisions of this section shall be commenced within thirty days after the commission of the offence.

As amended by Acts of 1906, Chap. 314,

Closed season on trout, land-locked salmon and lake trout.

SECTION 62. Whoever takes a trout, land-locked salmon or lake trout between the first day of August and the fifteenth day of April shall forfeit not less than ten nor more than twenty-five dollars for each offence. Whoever buys such fish taken between said dates in this commonwealth or takes fish with a net or salmon pot at any season of the year shall forfeit not less than five nor more than twenty dollars for each fish so taken.

As amended by Acts of 1906, Chap. 314.

Sale of wild trout, salmon, etc., prohibited.

SECTION 63. Whoever, except as provided in section sixty-six, sells or offers or exposes for sale, or has in his possession, a trout, land-locked salmon or lake trout, except alive, between the first day of August and the fifteenth day of April, shall forfeit not less than ten nor more than twenty-five dollars for each offence; and the possession of any such fish between said dates shall be prima facie evidence to convict.

SECTION 3. Nothing herein contained shall be construed as affecting or repealing the provisions of chapter two hundred and five of the acts of the year nineteen hundred and three.

SECTION 4. This act shall take effect on the thirty-first day of March in the year nineteen hundred and seven.

As amended by Acts of 1905, Chap. 190.

Illegal size of trout.

SECTION 64. Whoever at any time takes, catches or has in possession, or whoever sells or offers or exposes for sale in this commonwealth, trout less than six inches in length shall forfeit ten dollars for each such trout taken, caught, held in possession, sold or offered or exposed for sale; but the provisions of this section shall not affect the provisions of section twenty-eight, nor shall they apply to a person who is engaged in breeding or rearing trout or to any person who, upon taking such trout, immediately returns it alive to the water from which it was taken.

Public waters only to be stocked.

SECTION 65. No person, corporation or association shall be provided by the commonwealth with trout or trout spawn to stock waters owned or leased by him or them or under his or their control unless he or they first agree in writing with the commissioners on fisheries and game that such waters so stocked shall be free for the public to fish in during the season in which the taking of trout is permitted by law.

ACTS OF 1906, CHAP. 263.

Prohibition of the sale of all trout except those artificially reared.

SECTION 1. It shall be unlawful at any time within three years after April eighth, nineteen hundred and six, to buy or sell trout, or to offer trout for sale, within the commonwealth: *provided, however,* that nothing in this act shall prevent the sale of trout artificially propogated or maintained or hatched from the egg in the house of the owner and grown in pools of said owner, in so far as the sale thereof is permitted by the laws of this commonwealth now in force.

SECTION 2. Whoever violates any provision of this act shall be punished by a fine of one dollar for each trout so bought, sold or offered for sale.

SECTION 3. This act shall take effect on the eighth day of April in the year nineteen hundred and six.

AS AMENDED BY ACTS OF 1907, CHAP. 296.

Sale of artificially reared trout.

SECTION 66. Trout not less than nine inches in length, which are hatched from the egg in the house of the owner and grown in pools of said owner, may be sold for food from February first to April fifteenth.

AS AMENDED BY ACTS OF 1904, CHAP. 329.

PICKEREL.

Legal size of pickerel.

SECTION 67. Whoever takes from the waters of this commonwealth a pickerel less than ten inches in length, or sells or offers for sale, or has in his possession, with intent to sell any such pickerel, shall forfeit one dollar for each pickerel so taken, held in possession, sold or offered or exposed for sale; and in prosecutions under the provisions of this section the possession of pickerel less than ten inches in length shall be prima facie evidence to convict.

ACTS OF 1905, CHAP. 417.

Apparatus of capture.

SECTION 1. A town may by a by-law duly enacted and approved as required by law forbid the taking or catching of pickerel in any river, stream or pond therein in any other manner than by naturally or artificially baited hook and hand line, and may provide a suitable penalty for the violation of such by-law.

SECTION 2. Section sixty-eight of chapter ninety-one of the Revised Laws, and chapter three hundred and sixty-four of the acts of the year nineteen hundred and four, are hereby repealed.

SECTION 3. This act shall take effect upon its passage.

ACTS OF 1901, CHAP. 158, AS AMENDED BY ACTS OF 1905, CHAP. 429.

FISHING IN LAKE QUINSIGAMOND, WORCESTER.

SECTION 1.   For a period of five years after the passage of this act no person shall fish, except for pickerel, in any manner whatsoever between the first day of September and the first day of April in each year in Lake Quinsigamond in the county of Worcester, or in its tributaries, above what is known as the Stringer dam, including Full Moon cove, Jordan pond and Newton pond commonly called Mud pond; and between the first day of April and the first day of September in each year during said period no person shall take from said lake or its tributaries as aforesaid any fish, except pickerel, in any manner except with a single hook and either a hand line or a line attached to a rod or pole held by hand, with bait, artificial fly or spoon.

SECTION 2.   Section 2 of said chapter is hereby amended by inserting after the word."fish", in the first line, the words: — except pickerel, — so as to read as follows: — *Section 2.*   No person shall take any fish, except pickerel, from said lake or its tributaries as aforesaid during said period of five years for the purpose of sale, trade or barter.

ACTS OF 1904, CHAP. 223.

BLACK BASS.

Black bass protection repealed.

SECTION 1.   Section sixty-nine of chapter ninety-one of the Revised Laws, relative to the taking of black bass, is hereby repealed.

Size.

SECTION 70.   Whoever takes or sells or offers for sale or has in his possession with intent to sell a black bass less than eight inches in length shall forfeit ten dollars for each fish so taken, sold or offered or exposed for sale; and in prosecutions under the provisions of this section the possession of a black bass less than eight inches in length shall be prima facie evidence to convict.

SMELTS.

Close season.

SECTION 71. Whoever, between the fifteenth day of March and the first day of June, sells or offers or exposes for sale or has in his possession a smelt taken between said dates in this commonwealth, shall forfeit one dollar for every such smelt; and the possession of a smelt between said dates shall be prima facie evidence to convict.

Apparatus allowed.

SECTION 72. Whoever takes a smelt in any other manner than by naturally or artificially baited hook and hand line shall, except as provided in section seventy-six, forfeit one dollar for each smelt so taken; and in all prosecutions under the provisions of this section the burden of proof shall be upon the defendant to show that smelts taken by him were legally caught.

Exceptions in certain counties.

SECTION 73. The provisions of the two preceding sections shall not apply to smelts taken in a seine or net in the counties of Bristol, Barnstable, Nantucket or Dukes county during the time and in the manner in which fishing is allowed for perch, herring or alewives.

Prohibited apparatus.

SECTION 74. No person shall set, draw, use or attempt to set, draw or use any net, seine, trap or device for catching smelts, other than a naturally or artificially baited hook, in the waters of Boston harbor, Hingham harbor, Weir river,

Weymouth Fore river, Weymouth Back river,
Neponset river, Charles river, Mystic river, or in
any cove, bay, inlet or tributary thereof; but the
provisions of this section shall not prohibit the
use of traps for catching lobsters.

What constitutes evidence.

SECTION 75.   Possession of any net, seine, trap
or device for catching fish, other than a naturally
or artificially baited hook, in or upon said harbors, rivers or tributaries, or on the banks of the
same, if adapted to the present catching of smelts
and apparently intended for that purpose, shall
be deemed prima facie evidence of a violation of
the provisions of the preceding section, and the
possession of any fresh smelts, not apparently
caught by the use of a hook, in or upon said harbors, rivers or tributaries, or on the banks of
the same, after sunset or under other circum-
stances of suspicion, shall be deemed prima facie
evidence that said smelts were caught contrary
to the provisions of the preceding section by the
person in whose possession they are found.

Penalties.

SECTION 76.   Whoever violates the provisions of section seventy-four or receives smelts
knowing or having reasonable cause to believe
that the same have been taken contrary to the
provisions of said section shall, for a first offence,
be punished by a fine of not less than fifty nor
more than two hundred dollars or by imprisonment for not less than six nor more than twelve
months, or by both such fine and imprisonment,
and, for a second offence, by both said fine and
imprisonment.

Right of search.

SECTION 77.   Any commissioner on fisheries
and game, deputy commissioner, member of the
district police, sheriff, deputy sheriff, police

officer or constable, within his jurisdiction, may search for and seize, without warrant, any smelts which he has reason to suspect were taken contrary to the provisions of section seventy-four, and the net, seine, trap or other device and the vessel, boat, craft or other apparatus used in connection with such receiving, or other violation of said section, and the cask, barrel or other vessel or wrapper containing said smelts. Said officer may libel said property according to law, or, at his discretion, sell the same or any part thereof at private sale or by public auction, and libel the net proceeds of such sale according to law, in the same manner and with the same effect as if such proceeds were the property itself.

FORFEITURE OF FISH, BOATS, ETC.

Forfeiture of boats and apparatus.

SECTION 78. Whoever takes any fish in violation of the provisions of section twenty-six, twenty-nine, thirty-two, thirty-three, thirty-nine, forty, forty-two, forty-three, forty-four, forty-seven, fifty-eight, sixty-two, sixty-eight, sixty-nine, seventy-two, or one hundred and thirty-two, or whoever violates the provisions of sections twenty-six, thirty-three or seventy-six shall, in addition to the penalties therein provided, forfeit the boat and apparatus used.

Forfeiture of fish and apparatus.

SECTION 79. Whoever violates the provisions of sections twenty-six, thirty-two, forty-one, forty-eight, forty-nine, fifty-two and fifty-nine shall, in addition to the penalties therein provided, forfeit the fish taken and the apparatus used.

Duty of superintendents, clerks and others.

SECTION 80. Every superintendent, clerk or other person who has charge of a market, provision store or other place in which fish are sold, and who has reasonable cause to believe that any fish taken in violation of law has been offered for sale on such premises, shall immediately give information thereof to a constable or trial justice in the city or town in which said premises are situated; and for each neglect so to do shall be punished by a fine of not less than five nor more than fifty dollars.

PIKE PERCH.

Acts of 1908, Chap. 488.

Relative to pike perch caught in certain waters.

SECTION 1. No corporation, association or person shall have in possession in this commonwealth any pike perch caught in that part of Lake Champlain or its tributaries known as Missisquoi bay, lying and being in the province of Quebec, or in the Richelieu river, which is the outlet of said lake, between February first and June first.

SECTION 2. The commissioners on fisheries and game and their deputies are hereby authorized to search for, to seize, and to confiscate, without a warrant, pike perch held in possession in violation of the preceding section, and it shall be the duty of every officer designated in section four of chapter ninety-one of the Revised Laws, thus without a warrant to search for and seize pike perch so held in possession, and to report the seizure to the said commissioners, who shall authorize the sale of such fish; and the proceeds of such sale shall be paid into the treasury of the commonwealth.

SECTION 3. Any company, association or person violating the provisions of this act shall be liable to a penalty of fifty dollars, and ten dollars additional for each pike perch held in possession in violation of the provisions of this act. Chapter one hundred and seventy-nine of the acts of the year nineteen hundred and six is hereby repealed.

SHINERS AND STURGEON.

ACTS OF 1906, CHAP. 239.

The taking of shiners for bait.

SECTION 1.   It shall be lawful to take shiners for bait in any of the waters of the commonwealth by means of a circular or hoop net not exceeding 6 feet in diameter, or by means of a rectangular net other than a seine, containing not more than 36 square feet of net surface.

SECTION 2.   The provisions of section twenty-six of chapter ninety-one of the Revised Laws, as amended by chapter three hundred and eight of the acts of the year nineteen hundred and four, and of section one hundred and thirty-two of said chapter ninety-one, shall not apply to a person taking fish other than shiners by means of the apparatus described in section one: *provided,* that such other fish are immediately returned alive to the water.

SECTION 3.   This act shall take effect upon its passage.

AS AMENDED BY ACTS OF 1905, CHAP. 181.

Taking shiners for bait in the Merrimac and Connecticut rivers.

SECTION 81.   During October and November any person may, for the purpose of taking shiners for bait, draw a net or seine at any point in the Merrimac and Connecticut rivers and their tributaries, except within four hundred yards of any fishway; and if any other fish so caught are immediately returned alive to the waters from which they were taken, the penalties prescribed in sections forty-six, forty-seven, forty-nine, seventy-eight and seventy-nine shall not apply to the taking of such fish.

Sturgeon nets.

SECTION 82.   A person who uses a net or seine having a mesh which stretches at least twelve inches shall not incur a penalty for taking sturgeon in the tidal waters of the Merrimac river.

EELS, CLAMS, QUAHAUGS AND SCALLOPS.

SECTION 83, AS AMENDED BY ACTS OF 1908, CHAP. 270.

Relative to the taking of scallops.

SECTION 83. Whoever between the first day of April and the first day of October takes scallops from the flats or waters of the commonwealth by means of dredges, rakes, hoes, shovels or any other implement whatever, or buys or sells scallops so taken, or has them in possession for any purpose, shall be punished by a fine of not less than twenty nor more than fifty dollars for each offence; but the provisions of this section shall not apply to the taking of scallops for bait in the waters adjacent to the town of Nantucket from the first day of April to the fifteenth day of May inclusive.

SECTION 2. It shall be lawful for any person at any time to take scallops by hand for food for his own personal or family use.

ACTS OF 1907, CHAP. 297.

Protection of seed scallops.

SECTION 1. For the purposes of this act a seed scallop shall be a scallop with a bright, thin, slightly curved shell, with no foreign growth adherent, the shell having no sharply defined growth line, and the animal being less than one year old.

SECTION 2. No unculled or seed scallops taken from the flats or tide-waters of the Commonwealth shall be held in captivity. Seed scallops so taken shall be culled out and returned alive and uninjured to tide water which is at least three feet deep at mean low tide.

SECTION 3. Whoever takes or has in possession a seed scallop taken from the flats or tide waters of the Commonwealth and fails to return it immediately to tide water as provided in the preceding section, shall be punished by a fine of not less than five nor more than twenty dollars for each offence. Possession of a seed scallop shall be prima facie evidence that such seed scallop was taken from the flats or tide waters of the Commonwealth contrary to law.

SECTION 4. All acts and parts of acts inconsistent herewith are hereby repealed.

City and town jurisdiction.

SECTION 85. The mayor and aldermen of cities and the selectmen of towns, if so instructed by their cities and towns, may, except as provided in the two preceding sections, control, regulate or prohibit the taking of eels, clams, quahaugs and scallops within the same; and may grant permits prescribing the times and methods of taking eels and such shellfish within such cities and towns and make such other regulations in regard to said fisheries as they may deem expedient. But an inhabitant of the commonwealth, without such permit, may take eels and the shellfish above-named for his own family use from the waters of his own or any other city or town, and may take from the waters of his own city or town any of such shellfish for·bait, not exceeding three bushels, including shells, in any one day, subject to the general rules of the mayor and aldermen and selectmen, respectively, as to the times and methods of taking such fish. The provisious of this section shall not authorize the taking of fish in violation of the provisions of sections forty-four and forty-five. Whoever takes any eels or any of said shellfish without such permit, and in violation of the provisions of this section, shall forfeit not less than three nor more than fifty dollars.

ACTS OF 1904, CHAP. 269.

Quahaugs in Eastham, Orleans and Wellfleet.

SECTION 1. No person shall take quahaugs from their natural beds, or wilfully obstruct or interfere with such natural beds, within the towns

of Eastham, Orleans and Wellfleet, except as
hereinafter provided.

SECTION 2. No inhabitant of said towns shall
sell or offer for sale little neck clams or quahaugs
which measure less than one and one half inches
across the widest part, and no person shall in any
of said towns sell or offer for sale little neck clams
or quahaugs which measure less than one and
one half inches across the widest part.

SECTION 3. The selectmen of any one of said
towns may give to any inhabitants of any of said
towns permits in writing to take quahaugs from
their beds in the town which the selectmen rep-
resent at such times, in such quantities and for
such uses as they shall deem expedient. Such
permits shall be good for such time as the selectmen may determine, not exceeding one year.
Any inhabitant of the commonwealth may without such permit take from the natural beds in said
towns quahaugs for the use of his family, not
exceeding in quantity one bushel, including shells,
in any one day; and any fisherman may without
such permit take quahaugs from the natural beds
in his own town for bait for his own use, not exceeding in quantity one bushel, including shells,
in any one day.

SECTION 4. The selectmen of the said towns
may, in their respective towns, grant licenses or
permits for such periods, not exceeding two
years, and under such conditions as they may
deem proper, not however covering more than
seventy-five feet square in area, to any inhabitants of the town to bed quahaugs in any waters,
flats and creeks within the town at any place
where there is no natural quahaug bed, not impairing the private rights of any person or materially obstructing any navigable waters. It shall
be unlawful for any person, except the licensee
and his agents, to take any quahaugs in or remove them from the territory covered by any
such license.

SECTION 5. Whoever violates any provision

of this act or of any regulation made by the selectmen under authority hereof shall be punished by a fine of not more than one hundred dollars or by imprisonment for not more than six months, or by both such fine and imprisonment.

SECTION 6 [as amended by Acts of 1905, Chap. 265]. So much of section eighty-five of chapter ninety-one of the Revised Laws as is inconsistent herewith shall not apply to the said towns; and nothing herein contained shall be construed to affect the rights of the inhabitants of Orleans and Eastham under section five of chapter sixty-four of the acts of the year seventeen hundred and ninety-six, approved March third, seventeen hundred and ninety-seven.

SECTION 7. This act shall take effect in any of said towns only upon its acceptance by a majority of the voters thereof present and voting thereon at a meeting called for the purpose.

ACTS OF 1904, CHAP. 282.

Cultivation of shellfish.

SECTION 1. Cities by a two thirds vote of each branch of the city council in cities having a common council and a board of aldermen, or by a two thirds vote of the board of aldermen in cities not having a common council, and towns by a two thirds vote of the voters present and voting thereon at any town meeting called for the purpose, may appropriate money for the cultivation, propagation and protection of shellfish. The mayor and aldermen of cities, and the selectmen of towns, when so authorized by their respective cities and towns, may declare from time to time a close season for shellfish for not more than three years in such waters or flats within the limits of their respective cities and towns as they deem proper, and may plant and grow shellfish in such waters and flats : *provided*, that no private rights are impaired; and *provided, further*, that when any close season, declared as aforesaid, shall have ended, the flats and waters so closed shall be opened subject to the provisions of section eighty-five of chapter ninety-one of the Revised Laws, and of any special laws.

SECTION 2. Whoever takes shellfish in violation of the provisions of this act shall forfeit not less than three nor more than fifty dollars. Any officer qualified to serve criminal process, and special constables, designated under the provisions of section one hundred and thirty-four of chapter ninety-one of the Revised Laws, shall have power to enforce the provisions of this act, with all the powers conferred by said section.

SECTION 3. District courts and trial justices shall have concurrent jurisdiction with the superior court of all offences under this act.

ACTS OF 1906, CHAP. 477.

Protection of shellfish in the town of Dartmouth.

SECTION 1. No person shall take any shellfish from their beds or wilfully obstruct the growth of any shellfish within the town of Dartmouth, except as is hereinafter provided.

SECTION 2. The selectmen of said town may give permits in writing to any person to take shellfish from their beds within said town at such times, in such quantities, for such uses and by such methods as they shall deem expedient. They shall grant such permits to any inhabitant of the town to take from the beds in said town shellfish for the use of himself and his family not exceeding in quantity one half bushel including shells in any one day. They shall grant such permits to any fisherman to take shellfish from said beds for bait for his own use not exceeding in quantity one bushel including shells in any one day. Such permits shall be signed by the selectmen, shall be recorded in a book kept for the purpose and shall remain in force for one year from their date.

SECTION 3. Every person taking shellfish

from their beds within said town under the provisions of this act shall at the time of such taking have with him the permit granted to him as above provided and shall exhibit it upon demand to any constable of the town or other officer charged with the duty of enforcing the provisions of this act.

SECTION 4. No person shall take from their beds in said town or sell or offer for sale or have in his possession any little neck clams or quahaugs measuring less than one and one half inches across the widest part.

SECTION 5. Whoever violates any provision of this act shall be punished by a fine of not less than ten or more than one hundred dollars.

SECTION 6. The third district court of Bristol shall have concurrent jurisdiction with the superior court of all offences under this act.

SECTION 7. So much of section eighty-five of chapter ninety-one of the Revised Laws as is inconsistent herewith shall not apply to the town of Dartmouth.

LOBSTERS, TAUTOG AND OTHER FISH.

Egg lobsters.

SECTION 86. Whoever at any time catches or takes or has in his possession with intent to sell, or sells, any female lobster bearing eggs shall be punished by a fine of not less than ten nor more than one hundred dollars or by imprisonment for not less than one nor more than three months for each offence; but a person who catches or takes any such lobster and immediately returns it alive to the waters from which it was taken shall not be subject to such penalty. The provisions of this section shall not apply to lobsters spawning in lobster cars if they are immediately returned alive to the waters from which they were taken. Exposure for sale or possession otherwise than as herein provided shall be prima facie evidence of an intent to sell.

Town officers to enforce preceding section.

SECTION 87. The mayor and aldermen of cities, the selectmen of towns, police officers and constables shall cause the provisions of the preceding section to be enforced in their respective cities and towns.

AS AMENDED BY ACTS OF 1907, CHAP. 303.

Legal length of lobsters.

SECTION 88. Whoever sells or offers for sale or has in his possession an uncooked lobster less than nine inches in length, or a cooked lobster less than eight and three quarters inches in length, measuring from the extremity of the bone protruding from the head to the end of the bone of the middle flipper of the tail of the lobster, extended on its back its natural length, shall forfeit not more than five dollars for every such lobster, one half to the use of the city or town in which the offence is committed and one half to the commonwealth; and in all prosecutions under the provisions of this section any mutilation of a lobster, cooked or uncooked, which affects its measurement shall be prima facie evidence that the lobster is less than the required length and the possession of any lobster, cooked or uncooked, which is not of the required length shall be prima facie evidence to convict.

SECTION 2. This act shall take effect upon its passage.

Mutilation unlawful.

SECTION 89. Whoever, before a lobster is cooked, mutilates it by severing the tail from the body, or has such tail in possession, shall be punished by a fine of five dollars for each offence; and in all prosecutions under the provisions of this section the possession, by any person, of the tail of any uncooked lobster so severed from the body shall be prima facie evidence to convict.

Detail of district police.

SECTION 90. The governor, upon the written request of the commissioners on fisheries and game or one of them, may detail one or more of the district police from any district or town to enforce the provisions of section eighty-eight.

Right of search.

SECTION 91. For the purpose of enforcing the provisions of section eighty-eight, any one of the commissioners on fisheries and game or their deputy or any member of the district police may search in suspected places for, seize and remove lobsters which have been unlawfully taken, held or offered for sale.

Residence.

SECTION 92. Whoever, not having been an inhabitant of this commonwealth for one year, sets or keeps or causes to be set or kept in the waters of this commonwealth any pot, net or trap for the catching of lobsters shall forfeit twenty dollars for each offence.

Commissioners' rights.

SECTION 93. The commissioners on fisheries and game may occupy and use any small estuaries or creeks within the commonwealth, not exceeding six, for the scientific investigation of the habits, propagation and distribution of lobsters, if such occupation and use does not impair the private rights of any person or materially obstruct any navigable waters. Notice of such occupation shall be conspicuously posted and maintained by said commissioners at the nearest points to said estuaries and creeks, and shall be recorded in the registry of deeds in the county in which they are situated.

Penalty.

SECTION 94. Whoever, after the posting and recording of such notice, catches or takes any lobster from any estuary or creek so occupied as aforesaid shall be punished as provided in section eighty-six.

Non-residential prohibition upon taking lobsters and fish in Fairhaven, New Bedford, Dartmouth and Westport.

SECTION 95. No person living without this commonwealth shall take any lobsters, tautog, bass or other fish within the harbors, streams or waters of Fairhaven, New Bedford, Dartmouth or Westport for the purpose of carrying them thence in vessels or smacks of any size whatever owned without this commonwealth, nor in any of more than fifteen tons burden owned within this commonwealth, under a penalty of ten dollars for each offence and a forfeiture of all fish and lobsters so taken.

Territorial definition.

SECTION 96. For the purposes of the preceding section, the waters and shores of the places therein mentioned shall be deemed to extend from the line of the state of Rhode Island to the line of the county of Plymouth, and to include all the waters, islands and rocks lying within one mile of the mainland.

Penalty.

SECTION 97. If, within the harbors, streams, or waters of any place on the sea coast which accepts the provisions of this section or has accepted the corresponding provisions of earlier laws, a person who lives without the commonwealth takes, for the purpose of carrying thence, any lobsters, tautog, bass, bluefish or scuppaug, or if a person who lives in this commonwealth takes and carries away from such place any such fish or lobsters in vessels or smacks of more than fifteen tons burden, he shall forfeit for each offence not more than twenty dollars, and all the fish and lobsters so taken.

Transportation from Provincetown.

SECTION 98. No person shall take lobsters within the waters and shores of the town of Provincetown for the purpose of carrying them from said waters in a vessel or smack of more than fifteen tons burden, or for the purpose of putting them on board of such vessel or smack to be transported to any place, unless a permit is first obtained therefor from the selectmen of said town, who may grant the same for such amount, to be paid to the use of the town, as they shall deem proper. Whoever violates the provisions of this section shall forfeit ten dollars for each offence; and a further amount of ten dollars for every hundred lobsters over the first hundred taken or found on board of any such vessel or smack, and in that proportion for any smaller number. For the purposes of this section, the waters and shores of Provincetown shall be deemed to be as follows: beginning at Race Point, one half mile from the shore, and thence running by said shore to the end of Long Point which forms the harbor of Provincetown, and from the end of Long Point one half mile and including the harbor within the town of Provincetown.

Limitation in Buzzard's bay.

SECTION 99. Whoever, between the first day of April and the first day of July, inclusive, takes more than one hundred pounds a week of lobsters, tautog, bass or scuppaug in the bays, harbors, ponds, rivers or creeks of the waters of Buzzard's bay, within one mile from the shore and within the jurisdiction of the towns of Bourne and Wareham, shall forfeit not more than fifty dollars.

Authorizing purchase of egg-bearing lobsters, etc.

SECTION 1. The commissioners on fisheries and game are hereby authorized and empowered to purchase, at a rate not exceeding twenty-five per cent above the market price, lobsters with eggs attached, caught along the shore of this commonwealth. Whoever catches any such lobsters with eggs attached may, after receiving a permit from the commissioners on fisheries and game, safely store the same in lobster cars or sections of cars used for that purpose only, and may keep them separate from other lobsters until such time as the said commissioners or some person or persons designated by them can gather and pay for them. The commissioners and their agent shall liberate them in the vicinity of the location where they were caught; or they may at their discretion sell any portion or all of them to the officer in charge of the United States fish hatchery for artificial propagation, the proceeds to be applied to the appropriation made for the enforcement of this act.

OYSTERS AND OTHER SHELLFISH.

Oysters.

SECTION 100. Whoever takes oysters from their beds, or destroys them or wilfully obstructs their growth therein, except as is provided in the following sections, shall forfeit two dollars for every bushel of oysters, including the shells, so taken or destroyed.

Town officials may grant permits.

SECTION 101. The mayor and aldermen of a city or selectmen of a town in which there are oyster beds may grant a permit in writing to any person to take oysters from their beds at such times, in such quantities and for such uses as they shall express in their permit; but every inhab-

itant of such city or town, except the town of
Yarmouth, may, without such permit, take
oysters from the beds therein for the use of his
family, from the first day of September to the
first day of June, not exceeding in any week two
bushels, including the shells.

Penalties and permits.

SECTION 102.   Whoever takes any other shellfish from their beds, or destroys them or wilfully
obstructs their growth therein, except as is hereinafter provided, shall forfeit one dollar for
every bushel of such other shellfish, including
the shells.   But the mayor and aldermen of a
city or selectmen of a town may at any time give
a permit in writing to any person to take such
other shellfish from their beds therein, at such
times, in such quantities and for such uses as
they shall express in their permit; but every inhabitant of each of said places may, without such
permit, take such other shellfish from the beds
therein for the use of his family.

Rights of Indians and fishermen.

SECTION 103.   The provisions of the three preceding sections shall not deprive native Indians
of the privilege of digging shellfish for their own
consumption, or prevent a fisherman, who is an
inhabitant of this commonwealth, from taking
shellfish which he may want for bait, not exceeding at any one time seven bushels, including the
shells.

Oyster licenses.

SECTION 104.   The mayor and aldermen of a
city or selectmen of a town may, by writing under
their hands, grant a license for a term not exceeding ten years to any inhabitant thereof to
plant, grow and dig oysters at all times of the
year, or to plant oyster shells for the purpose of
catching oyster seed, upon and in any waters,
flats and creeks therein, at any place where

there is no natural oyster bed; not, however, impairing the private rights of any person, nor materially obstructing any navigable waters.

Limits of areas.

SECTION 105. Such license shall describe by metes and bounds the waters, flats and creeks so appropriated and shall be recorded by the city or town clerk before it shall have any force, and the licensee shall pay to the mayor and aldermen or selectmen, for their use, two dollars, and to the clerk fifty cents. The shore line of such licensed premises shall be the line of mean low water for the planting and growing of oysters, and the line of high water for the planting of oyster shells, but the provisions of this section shall not authorize the placing of such shells upon the land of a riparian owner between high and low water mark without his written consent.

Public hearings.

SECTION 106. Such license shall not be granted until after a public hearing, due notice of which shall have been posted in three or more public places in the city or town in which the premises are situated at least seven days before the time fixed for such hearing.

Who can have a license.

SECTION 107. Such license shall be granted, assigned or transferred only to inhabitants of the city or town in which the licensed premises are situated, and shall not be assigned or transferred without the written consent of the mayor and aldermen of such city or the selectmen of such town.

Rights of licensee.

SECTION 108. The licensee, his heirs and assigns shall, for the purposes aforesaid, have the exclusive use of the waters, flats and creeks

described in the license during the time therein
specified; and may, in an action of tort, recover
treble damages of any person who, without his or
their consent, digs or takes oysters or oyster
shells from such waters, flats or creeks during the
continuance of the license; and whoever digs or
takes oysters or oyster shells therefrom without
such consent shall also forfeit twenty dollars for
each offence.

Revocation of license.

SECTION 109. If the licensee fails for two
years after the license has been granted to plant
and grow oysters or to plant oyster shells in the
waters, flats or creeks described in the license, it
shall be revoked by the officers who granted it
and the revocation shall be recorded by the city
or town clerk.

Prohibition of night fishing.

SECTION 110. No person shall dig, take or
carry away any oysters or oyster shells between
one hour after sunset and one hour before sunrise, by any method whatever, from any waters,
flats or creeks for which a license has been granted
under the provisions of section one hundred and
four. . A licensee who violates the provisions of
this chapter relative to the planting and growing
of oysters or the planting of oyster shells, shall,
in addition to the penalties hereinafter provided,
forfeit his license and the oysters remaining on
the licensed premises.

Penalties.

SECTION 111. Whoever violates the provisions
of the preceding section, or whoever, without the
consent of the licensee, digs or takes any oysters
or oyster shells from any waters, flats or creeks
described in any license granted under the provisions of section one hundred and four, during
the continuance of such license, shall be punished

by a fine of not more than one hundred dollars
or by imprisonment for not less than thirty days
nor more than six months, or by both such fine
and imprisonment.

Trespass forbidden.

SECTION 112. Whoever works a dredge,
oyster tongs or rakes, or any other implement for
the taking of shellfish of any description, upon
any oyster grounds or beds, other than public
grounds or beds, without the consent of the
licensee, lessee or owner thereof, or whoever,
while upon or sailing over any such grounds or
beds, casts, hauls. or has overboard any such
dredge, tongs, rake or other implement for the
taking of shellfish of any description, under any
pretence or for any purpose whatever, without
the consent of the licensee, lessee or owner, shall,
for the first offence, be punished by a fine of not
more than twenty dollars or by imprisonment for
not more than thirty days, and for each subsequent offence, by a fine of not more than fifty
dollars or by imprisonment for not more than six
months.

Pollution.

SECTION 113. The state board of health may
examine all complaints which may be brought to
its notice relative to the contamination of tidal
waters and flats in this commonwealth by sewage
or other causes, may determine, as nearly as may
be, the bounds of such contamination, and, if
necessary, mark such bounds. It may also, in
writing, request the commissioners on fisheries
and game to prohibit the taking from such contaminated waters and flats of any oysters, clams,
quahaugs and scallops. Upon receipt of such
request, said commissioners shall prohibit the
taking of such shellfish from such contaminated
waters or flats for such period of time as the state
board of health may prescribe.

ACTS OF 1907, CHAP. 285.

The taking from contaminated waters of clams and quahaugs for bait.

SECTION 1. Whenever, upon the request of the state board of health under the provisions of section one hundred and thirteen of chapter ninety-one of the Revised Laws, the commissioners on fisheries and game have prohibited or may hereafter prohibit the taking from contaminated waters or flats in any city or town of any clams or quahaugs, the board of health of such city or town may grant permits in writing to any person to take from such waters clams or quahaugs to be used for bait only, and in such quantities and upon such conditions as they shall express in their permit.

SECTION 2. Any person holding a permit from the board of health of a city or town shall keep in his possession, and on his person, while acting thereunder, any permit obtained by him from said board of health, and shall at all times display the same upon the request of any person authorized to enforce the provisions of this act. Violation of this section shall be punished by a fine of not less than ten dollars nor more than fifty dollars, and in addition the permit shall be revoked and shall not thereafter be issued within twelve months.

SECTION 3. Any person who violates any of the provisions of such permit shall forfeit the permit and shall be punished by a fine not exceeding one hundred dollars, or by imprisonment for a term not exceeding three months, or by both such fine and imprisonment.

SECTION 4. Whoever sells, or exchanges, or exposes or offers for sale or exchange, or buys any clams or quahaugs, taken under the provisions of this act, shall be punished by a fine of not more than one hundred dollars, or by imprisonment for a term not exceeding three months, or by both such fine and imprisonment.

Penalties.

SECTION 114. Whoever takes any oysters, clams, quahaugs or scallops from tidal waters or flats from which the taking has been prohibited as provided in the preceding section shall forfeit not less than five nor more than ten dollars for the first offence, and not less than fifty nor more than one hundred dollars for each subsequent offence; but such penalties shall not be incurred until one week after the commissioners on fisheries and game shall have caused notice of such prohibition, with a description, or the bounds, of the tidal waters or flats to which such prohibition applies, to be published in a newspaper published in the town or county in which or adjacent to which the tidal waters or flats to which such prohibition applies are situated.

Shellfish for bait.

SECTION 115. No person shall take from the towns of Chatham, Nantucket, Barnstable or Mashpee any shellfish for bait or other use, except clams and a shellfish commonly known by the name of horsefeet; and no quantity exceeding seven bushels of clams, including the shells, or one hundred horsefeet, shall be taken in one week for each vessel or craft, nor, in any case, unless a permit has first been obtained from the selectmen of the town.

ACTS OF 1903, CHAP. 216.

Protection of shellfish, Edgartown.

SECTION 1. No person shall take any shellfish from their beds or wilfully obstruct the growth of any shellfish within the town of Edgartown, except as is hereinafter provided.

SECTION 2. The selectmen of said town may give permits in writing to any person to take shellfish from their beds within said town, at such times, in such quantities, and for such uses, as they shall deem expedient. But any inhabitant of said town may without such permit take from the beds in said town shellfish for the use of his family, not exceeding in quantity one bushel, including shells, in any one day; and any fisherman may without such permit take shellfish from the said beds for bait for his own use, not exceeding in quantity one bushel, including shells, in any one day.

SECTION 3. No person shall take from their beds in said town, or sell or offer for sale, or have in his possession, any little neck clams or quahaugs measuring less than one and one half inches across the widest part.

SECTION 4. Whoever violates any provision of this act shall be punished by a fine of not less than ten nor more than one hundred dollars.

SECTION 5 The district court of Dukes County shall have concurrent jurisdiction with the superior court of all offences under this act.

SECTION 6. So much of section eighty-five of chapter ninety-one of the Revised Laws as is inconsistent herewith shall not apply to the town of Edgartown.

REGULATION OF FISH WEIRS, NETS, PURSE AND SWEEP SEINES.

Authority to construct.

SECTION 116. The mayor and aldermen of a city and the selectmen of a town lying upon tide water, except cities and towns bordering on Buzzard's bay, may in writing authorize any person to construct weirs, pound nets or fish traps in said waters within the limits of such city or town for a term not exceeding five years, if such wiers, pound nets or fish traps do not obstruct navigation or encroach on the rights of other persons.

Penalty for injury.

SECTION 117. Whoever wilfully destroys or injures any such weir, pound net or fish trap, or takes fish therefrom without the consent of the owner, shall forfeit not more than twenty dollars to the use of the owner, and shall be liable in an action to the person injured.

Penalty for non-authorized construction.

SECTION 118. Whoever constructs or maintains a weir, pound net or fish trap in tide water without the authority mentioned in section one hundred and sixteen, or from an island in tide water without authority in writing from the mayor and aldermen of every city and the selectmen of every town which is distant not over two miles from said island, shall forfeit ten dollars for each day he maintains such weir, pound net or fish trap; and he may be indicted therefor and enjoined therefrom.

Statistical returns of fishing.

SECTION 119. The owner of every pound net, weir, fyke net or similar contrivance, of every fishing pier, seine, drag or gill net, lobster pot or trap used in any of the waters of this commonwealth for fishing purposes, shall annually, on or before the twentieth day of October, make 'a written report, under oath, to the commissioners of the number of pounds and the value of each kind of edible fish caught by his pound net, weir, fyke net or similar contrivance, pier, seine, drag or gill net, and the number and value of lobsters taken by him in pots or traps, during the year last preceding the date of said report, and the number and value of the devices used in such catching or taking, and the number of persons employed therein; and for such purpose, the commissioners shall annually, on or before the fifteenth day of March, provide him, upon his application, with suitable blank forms for such reports, so arranged that each month's catch may be separately recorded thereon; and, in filling out such reports, such owner shall give the results of each month's fishing, so far as may be practicable. Such owner shall apply to the commissioners for such blank forms. The owner of any cars or other contrivances used for keeping lobsters shall have his name and residence legibly marked thereon. Whoever knowingly and wilfully violates the provisions of this section shall be punished by a fine of not less than ten nor more than one hundred dollars.

Close time for net fishing.

SECTION 120. Subject to the provisions of the two following sections, no person shall, from the first day of May to the fifteenth day of June, set, or permit to remain set, a fish pound, weir, trap, fyke or similar fixed apparatus for catching fish, except gill nets, between the hours of six o'clock on Saturday morning and six o'clock on Sunday evening, so as to catch fish in the tidal waters of the counties of Dukes County or Bristol, of the towns of Mattapoisett, Marion or Wareham, of the westerly boundaries of Bourne and Falmouth at and near Buzzard's bay, or of that portion of the southerly boundary of the county of Barnstable extending from the southwesterly corner of the town of Falmouth easterly to Point Gammon in the town of Yarmouth. Whoever violates the provisions of this section shall be punished by a fine of not less than one hundred nor more than two hundred dollars; but all prosecutions under this section shall be commenced within three months after the commission of the offence.

Traps prohibited in Buzzard's bay.

SECTION 121. Whoever sets, uses or maintains any trap, weir, pound, yard or other stationary apparatus of any kind for the taking of fish in the waters of Buzzard's bay or in any harbor, cove or bight thereof shall be punished by a fine of not less than one hundred nor more than five hundred dollars, or by imprisonment for not more than six months.

Nets prohibited in Buzzard's bay.

SECTION 122. No person shall draw, set, stretch or use any drag net, set net or gill net, purse or sweep seine of any kind for taking fish in the waters of Buzzard's bay or in any harbor, cove or bight thereof within the jurisdiction of this commonwealth. Whoever violates, or aids or abets in the violation of, the provisions of this section shall be punished by a fine of not more than two hundred dollars for each offence.

Penalties.

SECTION 123. A net or seine which is used in violation of the provisions of the preceding section and a boat, craft or fishing apparatus which is employed in such illegal use, and all fish found therewith, shall be forfeited. An inhabitant of a town bordering on said bay may seize and detain for not more than forty-eight hours any net or seine found in use in violation of the provisions of the preceding section, and any boat, craft, fishing apparatus and fish found therewith, so that they may be seized and libelled.

When nets are nuisances.

SECTION 124. All nets and seines in actual use which are set or stretched in violation of the provisions of sections one hundred and twenty-two and one hundred and twenty-eight are declared to be common nuisances.

Fishing rights in Buzzard's bay.

SECTION 125. The provisions of the four preceding sections shall not affect the corporate rights of any fishing company situated on Buzzard's bay, nor the use of nets or seines in lawful fisheries for shad or alewives in influent streams of said bay.

Limits of Buzzard's bay.

SECTION 126. In the statutes of this commonwealth the term "waters of Buzzard's bay" shall
be deemed to mean the body of water commonly
known as Buzzard's bay and extending southwesterly to a line drawn from Cuttyhunk lighthouse to the southerly extremity of Gooseberry
neck in the town of Westport.

AS AMENDED BY ACTS OF 1905, CHAP. 281.

Restrictions, Edgartown and Cottage City.[1]

SECTION 127. Whoever sets or uses or aids in
setting or using any seine, mesh net or gill net for
the purpose of catching any other fish than mackerel, or by such means catches and retains any
other fish than mackerel, in the waters of the
towns of Edgartown and Cottage City[1] within
three miles from the shores thereof, may, upon
view of the offence by any of the commissioners
on fisheries and game or their deputies, or any
officers qualified to serve criminal process or member of the district police, be arrested without
warrant and prosecuted by him; and on conviction thereof shall be punished by a fine of not
more than two hundred dollars, and, in the discretion of the court, shall forfeit to the commonwealth all fish taken in said nets. The provisions of this section shall not affect the rights
of any persons mentioned in section twenty-three
or the corporate rights of any fishing company;
nor shall they prevent the inhabitants of said
towns from taking menhaden for bait for their
own use in the waters of their respective towns in
the months of July, August, September and October.

SECTION 2. This act shall not restrict or affect
the authority granted by chapter three hundred
and one of the acts of the year nineteen hundred

---

[1] Now Oak Bluffs.

and four to the selectmen of the town of Edgartown to issue certain permits for the taking of bait.

Prohibits the taking of fish by nets and seines in the waters of Barnstable and Mashpee on Nantucket sound.

SECTION 1. After the passage of this act no person shall draw, set, stretch or use any purse or sweep seine of any kind, except as is hereinafter provided, for taking fish anywhere in the waters of the towns of Barnstable or Mashpee on Nantucket Sound, so-called, northerly of or within a straight line extended from Point Gammon to Succonessett Point; nor in any bay, harbor, cove or bight of said waters, nor in any inlet or stream flowing into the same: *provided, however*, that nothing herein contained shall be so construed as to forbid or make unlawful the catching of menhaden or other small fish for bait purposes, nor the use of nets for the taking of herring, nor the use of dredges or drag nets for the taking of scallops.

SECTION 2. Whoever violates any provision of this act, or aids or assists in so doing, shall be punished by a fine of not less than fifty dollars nor more than five hundred dollars for each offence, or by imprisonment for a term not exceeding six months.

SECTION 3. Any net, seine or movable device for catching fish used in violation of any provision of this act, together with any boat, craft, vessel, steamer or fishing apparatus employed in such illegal use, and any fish found therewith, are hereby declared to be public nuisances and forfeited; and it shall be lawful for any inhabitant of said Barnstable or Mashpee, or any constable, police officer or deputy sheriff in the Commonwealth, to seize and detain, without warrant, for a period not exceeding forty-eight hours, any such net, seine or movable device, boat, craft, vessel, steamer or fishing apparatus found in use contrary to the provisions of this act, and any fish found therewith, to the end that the same may be libelled, if necessary, by due process of law. District courts and trial justices shall have concurrent jurisdiction with the superior court of all offences and proceedings under the provisions of this act, regardless of the value of the property libelled.

ACTS OF 1904, CHAP. 118.

Restrictions, Pleasant bay, Orleans.

SECTION 1. No purse or sweep seines, set nets or gill nets, for the taking of fish shall be set, drawn, used or maintained in the waters of Pleasant bay or its tributaries in the town of Orleans; but nothing herein contained shall be construed to forbid or make unlawful the maintaining of traps, pounds or weirs under licenses granted in accordance with section one hundred and sixteen of chapter ninety-one of the Revised Laws.

SECTION 2. Any person who shall set, draw, use or maintain a purse or sweep seine, set net or gill net in violation of this act shall be punished by a fine of not less than one hundred nor more than five hundred dollars, or by imprisonment for a term not exceeding six months.

SECTION 3. Chapter one hundred and sixty-three of the acts of the year nineteen hundred and one is hereby repealed.

AS AMENDED BY ACTS OF 1907, CHAP. 298.

Restrictions, Westport.

SECTION 128. Whoever draws, sets, stretches or uses any net, purse or seine of any kind for taking fish in the waters of Westport river between the first day of May and the first day of November shall be punished by a fine of not more than fifty dollars or by imprisonment for not more than three months, or by both such fine and imprisonment; and it shall be the duty of every officer designated in section four of this chapter to seize fish killed contrary to the provisions of this chapter and to report the seizure to the commissioners on fisheries and game, who shall authorize the sale of such fish; and the proceeds of any such sale, after paying the expenses thereof, shall be paid into the treasury of the commonwealth.

SECTION 2. Section one hundred and twenty-nine of said chapter ninety-one is hereby repealed.

Fish wardens, Westport.

SECTION 130. The town of Westport shall at each annual town election choose by ballot for a term of three years a person who shall be sworn to enforce the provisions of section one hundred and twenty-eight.

ACTS OF 1904, CHAP. 319.

Fish wardens, Edgartown.

The town of Edgartown is hereby authorized to choose at any annual town meeting, or at any meeting duly called for the purpose, fish wardens, in such number and with such compensation as the town may determine, who shall be sworn to the faithful discharge of their duty, which shall be to enforce the fishery laws in that town; and for this purpose the fish wardens so chosen shall have the powers which the district police now have or shall hereafter have for the enforcement of the fishery laws of the commonwealth.

ACTS OF 1904, CHAP. 301.

Regarding eel bait, Edgartown.

SECTION 1. The selectmen of the town of Edgartown, or any two of them, may issue to any inhabitant of said town holding a permit for the taking of eels by means of pots, permits for

the taking of bait for his own use only from the
waters of said town by means of nets or seines.
Such permits shall not be issued for the use of nets
or seines more than one hundred and fifty feet
long, or of a size of mesh of more than three
fourths of an inch, and shall be issued for the
taking of such bait only between the first day of
June and the fifteenth day of December in each
year. The provisions of this act shall not affect
the rights of the persons designated in section
twenty-three of chapter ninety-one of the Revised Laws, or the corporate rights of any fishing
company.

SECTION 2. So much of section one hundred
and twenty-seven of chapter ninety-one of the
Revised Laws and of any other act as is inconsistent herewith is hereby repealed.

GENERAL PROVISIONS.

Penalty for robbing pots, trawls, etc.

SECTION 131. Whoever takes any fish or
lobster from a trap, trawl or seine net for catching
fish or lobsters, without the consent of the owner
thereof, and whoever wilfully molests or interferes with such trap, trawl or seine, shall, for the
first offence, be punished by a fine of not less than
five nor more than twenty-five dollars or by imprisonment for thirty days, or by both such fine
and imprisonment; and for any subsequent
offence, by a fine of not less than twenty nor more
than fifty dollars or by imprisonment for sixty
days, or by both such fine and imprisonment.

AS AMENDED BY ACTS OF 1908, CHAP. 492.

Apparatus for fresh water fishing.

SECTION 132. Whoever takes any fish which
at any season frequent fresh water, except as
otherwise allowed in this chapter, in any other
manner than by artificially or naturally baited
hook and hand line, shall forfeit not less than

five nor more than fifty dollars; but towns may permit the use of nets and seines for taking herring and alewives; and nothing in this act shall be construed to prohibit the spearing of that species of fish commonly known as "suckers."

As amended by Acts of 1903, Chap. 246.

For the better protection of fish.

SECTION 133. Whoever puts or throws into any waters for the purpose of taking or destroying fish therein any poisonous substance, simple, mixed or compound, or whoever kills or destroys fish by the use of dynamite or other explosive, or explodes dynamite or powder in fishing waters, shall forfeit ten dollars for each offence: *provided, however*, that the provisions of this act shall not apply to operations of the federal government, of the state government, or of any municipal government in this commonwealth, nor to the use of explosives for raising the body of a drowned person.

Shellfish constables.

SECTION 134. The mayor and aldermen of a city or the selectmen of a town may designate one or more constables for the detection and prosecution of any violation of the laws of the commonwealth relative to shell fisheries. Such constables may arrest without warrant any person found violating such laws, and detain him for prosecution not more than twenty-four hours; and may seize any boat or vessel used in such violation, and her tackle, apparel and furniture and implements, which shall be forfeited.

Time of prosecutions.

SECTION 135. Actions and prosecutions under the laws relative to fisheries shall, unless otherwise expressly provided, be commenced within one year after the time when the cause of action accrued or the offence was committed.

Duties of municipal officers, etc.

SECTION 136. The mayor and aldermen of cities, the selectmen of towns, police officers and constables shall cause the provisions of sections sixty-three, seventy-one and seventy-two to be enforced in their respective cities and towns.

ACTS OF 1908, CHAP. 330.

Disposition of fines recovered in prosecutions under the laws relating to fisheries, birds, animals and game.

SECTION 1. All fines, penalties and forfeitures recovered in prosecutions under the laws relative to fisheries or to birds, animals and game, except as provided in section eighty-eight of chapter ninety-one of the Revised Laws, as amended by section one of chapter three hundred and three of the acts of the year nineteen hundred and seven, shall be equally divided between the county in which such prosecution is made and the commonwealth: *provided, however,* that if the plaintiff is a deputy appointed by the commissioners on fisheries and game and is receiving compensation from the commonwealth, such fines, penalties and forfeitures shall be paid into the treasury of the commonwealth

SECTION 2. Section one hundred and thirty-seven of chapter ninety-one of the Revised Laws and section twenty of chapter ninety-two of the Revised Laws, as amended by chapter four hundred and forty-five of the acts of the year nineteen hundred and five and by chapter three hundred of the acts of the year nineteen hundred and seven, are hereby repealed.

SECTION 3. This act shall take effect upon its passage.

Special statutes not repealed.

SECTION 138. The provisions of this chapter shall not repeal or affect any provisions or penalties contained or any privileges granted in any special statutes relating to fisheries in particular places.

ACTS OF 1908, CHAP. 76.

The bounty on seals abolished.

SECTION 1. Section one hundred and thirty-nine of chapter ninety-one of the Revised Laws, establishing a bounty for killing seals, is hereby repealed.

KELP AND SEAWEED.

SECTION 140. Any person may take and carry away kelp or other seaweed between high and low water mark while it is actually adrift in tide waters; but for such purpose no person shall enter on upland or on lawfully enclosed flats without the consent of the owner or lawful occupant thereof. The provisions of this section shall not apply to any city or town in which the subject matter thereof is regulated by special laws.

GAME LAWS.

REVISED LAWS, CHAP. 92.

ACTS OF 1905, CHAP. 317, AS AMENDED BY ACTS OF 1908, CHAP. 402.

Unnaturalized, foreign born persons must procure license to hunt.

SECTION 1. It shall be unlawful for any unnaturalized, foreign born person to hunt, pursue, trap or kill any wild bird or quadruped anywhere within the limits of the commonwealth, unless he is licensed so to do as hereinafter provided.

SECTION 2. City and town clerks shall, upon the application of any unnaturalized, foreign born person who is a resident of the city or town in which the application is made, and upon the payment of a fee of fifteen dollars, issue to such person a license, upon a form to be supplied by the commissioners on fisheries and game, bearing the name, age and place of residence of the licensee, with a description of him, as near as may be, and authorizing the said licensee to hunt and to kill game on any lands in which such hunting or killing is not forbidden by law or by written or printed notices posted thereon by the owner, lessee or occupant thereof. Such license shall be good only for that period of the year when game may lawfully be killed, and shall authorize the hunting or killing of game only under such restrictions and for such purposes as are imposed or authorized by law. The said license shall not be transferable, shall expire on the thirty-first day of December of the year of issue, and shall be exhibited upon demand to any of the commissioners on fisheries and game or their deputies, and to any game warden or deputy game warden, and to any sheriff, constable, police officer or other officer qualified to serve process. The fees received for the said licenses shall an-

nually be paid into the treasury of the commonwealth.

SECTION 3.   A license granted hereunder shall
be revoked by the city or town clerk issuing the
same in case the licensee is convicted of a violation of the fish and game laws, or of hunting upon
Sunday in violation of law.

SECTION 4.   It shall be the duty of the commissioners on fisheries and game, upon request by
any city or town clerk, to supply such clerk with
license forms prepared in accordance with the
provisions of this act.

SECTION 5.   Whoever violates any provision
of this act shall be punished by a fine of not less
than ten nor more than fifty dollars.

ACTS OF 1907, CHAP. 198.

Non-resident hunters must procure licenses to
hunt.

SECTION 1.   If any person, not a bona fide
resident of this commonwealth and actually
domiciled therein for a period of six months,
shall hunt, pursue or kill, within the limits of this
commonwealth, any wild animal, wild fowl or
bird without having first procured of the commissioners on fisheries and game a license to so
hunt, pursue or kill, as hereinafter provided, he
shall be fined, for each offence, a sum not exceeding fifty dollars, or be imprisoned for a term
not exceeding thirty days, or shall suffer both
such fine and imprisonment; and the same penalties shall be imposed upon any such person who
shall be convicted of so hunting, pursuing or
killing such wild animal, wild fowl or bird on a
license which has been issued in the name of
another person.

SECTION 2.   For the purposes of this act, any
resident of another state who owns real estate
situated within this commonwealth which is
assessed for taxation at a value of not less than
five hundred dollars shall have the right to hunt
without a license.

SECTION 3.· The commissioners on fisheries and game may, upon application therefor, issue a license to a non-resident which shall entitle such person to the privileges enjoyed by residents of this commonwealth as to the hunting and killing of all wild animals, wild fowl or birds. Such license shall be recorded in detail in books kept for that purpose, shall not be transferable nor available to any person other than the one named therein, shall be valid and in force only during the calendar year in which it is issued and dated, and shall entitle the licensee to hunt and kill only during the respective periods of the year when it is lawful for residents to so hunt and kill. Such license shall state the name, age, color of hair and eyes, and residence of the applicant.

SECTION 4. No license shall be valid unless the signature of the person to whom it is issued is written thereon, and every such person shall at all times when hunting carry his license on his person, and shall at all reasonable times and as often as requested produce and show such license to any person requesting him so to do, and if he fails or refuses so to do he shall forfeit the license and be deemed to be hunting in violation of the provisions of this act.

SECTION 5. Each non-resident hunting license shall entitle the licensee to carry from the commonwealth not more than six wild fowl or birds of all kinds, the exportation of which is prohibited by law, in any one calendar year: *provided*, that the owner thereof shall carry them open to view for inspection, shall present his license for inspection upon demand, and shall have informed, by letter or otherwise, the commissioner who issued the license as to the number and kinds of wild fowl or birds which he intends to carry from the commonwealth. Whoever violates any provision of this section shall be fined not more than fifty dollars, or be imprisoned for not more than thirty days, or shall suffer both such fine and imprisonment.

SECTION 6. The commissioners on fisheries
and game, and the detectives in their employ,
shall have the right, after demand and refusal
or failure to exhibit any such license, to arrest
without warrant any non-resident person or persons found hunting, pursuing or killing any wild
animal, wild fowl or bird, and for the purpose of
this arrest any person who shall refuse to state
his name and place of residence on demand of
such officer shall be deemed a non-resident.

SECTION 7. The fee for the license aforesaid
shall be ten dollars, except as hereinafter provided, and the money so received by the said
commissioners shall be turned over to the treasurer and receiver general. The fee for said
license shall be one dollar to any non-resident
member of any club, organization or association
incorporated at the time of the passage of this
act for the purposes of hunting or fishing, if such
club, organization or association owns real estate
in this commonwealth which is assessed therein
for taxation at a valuation of not less than one
thousand dollars.

ACTS OF 1908, CHAP. 484.

The Registration of hunters.

SECTION 1. No citizen of the United States
resident in Massachusetts shall hunt, pursue,
take, or kill any bird or quadruped protected by
law without first having obtained a certificate of
registration as hereinafter provided: *provided,*
however, that nothing in this act shall be construed as affecting in any way the provisions
of the general laws relating to trespass, or as
authorizing the hunting, pursuing, taking, wounding, or killing, or the possession of birds or quadrupeds contrary to any laws now or hereinafter in
force, nor shall the possession of such certificate
of registration grant or confer any privilege not
enjoyed prior to the passage of this act.

SECTION 2. The clerk of any city or town shall,

upon the application of any such bona fide resident citizen and the payment of the registration fee and recording fee hereinafter provided, issue to such person a certificate in the form prescribed and upon blanks furnished by the commissioners on fisheries and game, which certificate shall bear the name, age, occupation, place of residence, signature and an identifying description of the person thus registered, and shall authorize the person so registered to hunt game birds and game quadrupeds during the period when the same, respectively, may lawfully be killed, and at no other time, and only subject to the restrictions and conditions as provided by law. Said certificates shall be valid until January first next following the date of issue and no longer, shall not be transferable, and shall be produced for examination upon demand of any commissioner of fisheries and game, or their deputies or upon demand of any sheriff, constable, police officer, or other officer authorized to arrest for crime, or of the owner or lessee in actual occupancy of any land upon which such registered person may be found. Failure or refusal to produce said certificate upon such demand shall be prima facie evidence of a violation of this act.

SECTION 3. Every citizen of the United States who is a bona fide resident of this state shall pay for such certificate a fee of one dollar: *provided, however,* that this act shall not apply to any such citizen who is a bona fide resident on land owned or leased by him and on which he is actually domiciled, which land is used exclusively for agricultural purposes, and not for club or shooting purposes.

SECTION 4. Every city and town clerk shall keep a record of all such certificates issued by him, which record shall be open to inspection by all officers authorized to make arrests, and by the state treasurer and the state auditor or their agents, and by the commissioners on fisheries and game and their deputies; and such clerk shall,

on the first Monday in every month, pay to the
state treasurer all money received by him for
such certificates issued during the month preceding.

SECTION 5. Any person who shall violate any
provision of this act shall be fined not less than
ten nor more than fifty dollars, or be imprisoned
for not more than thirty days, or shall be punished by both such fine and imprisonment; and
the certificate of any person who shall be convicted of a violation of any law relating to
birds or quadrupeds, or of any provision of this
act, shall be void, and such person shall not
receive a certificate during the period of one year
from the date of such conviction.

SECTION 6. This act shall take effect on the
first day of January in the year nineteen hundred
and nine.

As AMENDED BY ACTS OF 1904, CHAP. 176.

Lord's day close season.

SECTION 1. The Lord's day shall be close season. Whoever hunts or destroys birds, wild
animals or game of any kind on the Lord's day
shall be liable to a penalty of not less than ten
nor more than twenty dollars in addition to any
penalties for taking, killing or having in possession birds, wild animals or game protected by law.

ACTS OF 1908, CHAP. 441.

Ruffed grouse, woodcock and quail.

SECTION 1. It shall be unlawful, between the
first day of November and the first day of October following, to hunt, pursue, take or kill a
ruffed grouse, commonly called partridge, a
woodcock, or a quail, or to have the same, or
any part thereof, in possession, whenever or
wherever the bird may have been taken or killed.

SECTION 2. It shall be unlawful to buy, sell,
offer for sale or otherwise dispose of at any time
any of the above mentioned birds, or any part

thereof, whenever or wherever such bird may
have been taken or killed: *provided, however,*
that a person, firm or corporation dealing in
game, or engaged in the cold storage business,
may buy, sell or have in possession, and a person
may buy from such person, firm or corporation,
and may have in possession if so bought, quail
from the first day of November to the first day of
January following, if such quail or parts thereof
were not taken in this commonwealth, and were
not taken, killed, bought, sold or otherwise disposed of or transported contrary to the laws of
any state or country. And a person, firm or corporation dealing in game or engaged in the cold
storage business may have quail in possession in
cold storage for storage purposes, at any season,
if such quail were not taken or killed in this commonwealth, and were not taken, killed, bought,
sold or otherwise procured or disposed of, or
transported contrary to the laws of the state or
country in which the quail were taken, killed,
or transported; *provided, however,* that such persons, firms or corporations shall have notified in
writing the commissioners on fisheries and game
on or before January first in each year, of the
species, number of each species, and place of
storage of such birds, and that such birds are in
places and packages convenient for sealing, and
that the packages are plainly marked with the
name and number of the birds therein. The
commissioners or their deputies shall then place a
seal upon all receptacles and packages containing
any species of quail. The said seal shall not be
removed by any person other than the commissioners on fisheries and game or their deputies,
and shall be removed by the said commissioners
or their deputies upon the first day of November
of each year. The packages so sealed shall not
be opened or removed from that storage warehouse under a penalty of twenty dollars for each
bird. But any person, firm or corporation holding a permit from the commissioners on fisheries

and game may buy, sell, or have in possession
.live quail for purposes of propagation within the
commonwealth, and for no other purpose.

SECTION 3. Whoever violates any provision of
this act shall be punished by a fine of twenty dollars for each bird or part thereof, in respect to
which the violation occurs. The possession, except as provided above, of quail during the season
when taking, killing, or sale is prohibited by law
shall be prima facie evidence that the person
having possession has violated some provision of
this act.

SECTION 4. Section two of chapter ninety-two
of the Revised Laws, as amended by chapter two
hundred and six of the acts of the year nineteen
hundred and three, and chapter three hundred
and three of the acts of the year nineteen hundred
and six are hereby repealed.

ACTS OF 1905, CHAP. 122.

The protection of quail on the island of Nantucket.

SECTION 1. It shall be unlawful to take, kill
or have in possession any quail on the island of
Nantucket at any time within three years after
the first day of March in the year nineteen hundred and five.

SECTION 2. Whoever violates any provisions
or this act shall be punished by a fine of twenty
dollars for every quail taken, killed or had in
possession contrary to the provisions hereof.

ACTS OF 1907, CHAP. 118.

The protection of loons and eagles.

SECTION 1. It shall be unlawful to hunt, capture, wound or kill a loon in or upon fresh water,
or an eagle in any place.

SECTION 2. Whoever violates any provision
of this act shall be punished by a fine of twenty
dollars.

ACTS OF 1906, CHAP. 141.

To prevent the extermination of the heath hen, so called.

SECTION 1. It shall be unlawful to hunt, take or kill that species of pinnated grouse commonly called heath hen, and scientifically known as *Tympanuchus cupido*, or to buy, sell, or otherwise dispose of, or have in possession the same or any part thereof, previous to the first day of November in the year nineteen hundred and eleven.

SECTION 2. So much of section four of chapter ninety-two of the Revised Laws as is inconsistent herewith is hereby repealed.

SECTION 3. Whoever violates any provision of this act shall be punished by a fine of one hundred dollars for each bird or part thereof in respect to which such violation occurs.

SECTION 4. This act shall take effect five days after its passage.

ACTS OF 1907, CHAP. 504.

Authorizes the taking of certain unimproved land upon the island of Martha's Vineyard for the protection of pinnated grouse and other birds.

SECTION 1. The commissioners on fisheries and game are hereby authorized to take, or receive as a gift, or lease, for and in the name of the commonwealth such unimproved lands on the island of Martha's Vineyard, not exceeding one thousand acres, and such other property as they may deem necessary for the purpose of making fire stops for the protection from fire of the feeding and breeding grounds of the pinnated grouse, or of otherwise securing the maintenance and increase of the said birds, or of any other species of wild birds upon said island; and the control and use of the lands or other property so acquired or leased, or of any land or property otherwise placed under the temporary or permanent control of said commissioners for the said purposes shall be vested in said commissioners, and the provisions of chapter three hundred and twenty-seven of the acts of the year nineteen hundred and six shall apply thereto.

SECTION 2. Said commissioners shall, within thirty days after taking any land under this act, file and cause to be recorded in the office of the register of deeds for the county of Dukes County at Edgartown, a certificate describing by metes and bounds the land so taken, stating the names of the owners, so far as they may be known, and also stating the purpose of such taking as hereinbefore specified. Said plan and certificate shall be signed by said commissioners, or by a majority of them.

SECTION 3. Any person sustaining damages by the taking of land as herein provided, who fails to agree with said commissioners as to the amount thereof, may, on application at any time within one year after the taking of such land, have the same assessed and determined in the manner provided by law in the case of land taken for the laying out of highways.

SECTION 4. In any proceeding for the recovery of damages hereunder, said commissioners may offer in court and may consent in writing that the sum therein specified may be awarded to the complainant as damages, and if the complainant shall not accept the same within ten days after he has received notice of such offer and shall not finally recover a greater sum than that offered, not including interest on the sum recovered in damages from the date of the offer, said commissioners shall be entitled to recover costs after such date, and the complainant, if he recover damages, shall be allowed costs only to the date of the offer unless the damages so recovered shall be in excess of the amount offered as aforesaid by said commissioners.

SECTION 5. For the purpose of acquiring said lands as aforesaid, and for the preparation of said fire stops and for other work incidental to the purposes hereinbefore set forth, and for investi-

gating and reporting upon the best methods and
probable cost of protecting and increasing the
colonies of birds on the island, the sum of two
thousand dollars may be expended; and said
commissioners may also expend in accordance
with the provisions of this act such other sums
as towns, associations or individuals may from
time to time pay to the treasurer of the commonwealth for the said purposes.

ACTS OF 1906, CHAP. 304.

An act to prohibit the sale of prairie chickens.

SECTION 1. It shall be unlawful to buy, sell,
or otherwise dispose of, or to have in possession, a
prairie chicken, scientifically known as *Tympanuchus Americanus*, and as *Pedioecetes phasian-
ellus*, or any part thereof, whenever or wherever
taken.

SECTION 2. Whoever violates any provision
of this act shall be punished by a fine of twenty
dollars for each bird or part thereof, in respect
to which the violation occurs, and possession
shall be prima facie evidence that the person
having possession has violated the provisions of
this act.

SECTION 3. This act shall take effect on the
first day of January in the year nineteen-hundred
and seven.

ACTS OF 1906, CHAP. 274.

An act relative to the protection of wood or
summer duck.

SECTION 1. It shall be unlawful, prior to the
first day of September in the year nineteen hundred and eleven, to hunt, capture, wound or kill
a wood or summer duck.

SECTION 2. Whoever violates the provisions
of this act shall be punished by a fine of not more
than fifty dollars for each violation. The
possession of any wood duck or summer duck,
or any part thereof, shall be prima facie evidence
of a violation of the provisions of this act

ACTS OF 1906, CHAP. 301.

An act relative to ducks and teal.

SECTION 1.   It shall be unlawful to kill a black duck, scientifically known as *Anas obscura*, or a teal, between the first day of March and the first day of September following, or any species of wild duck, not otherwise protected by law, between the twentieth day of May and the first day of September, or to buy, sell or have in possession a black duck or teal, between the first day of March and the first day of September, or any of the wild duck species during the time within which the taking or killing thereof is prohibited, whenever or wherever such birds may have been taken or killed: *provided, however*, that any person, firm or corporation holding a permit from the commissioners on fisheries and game may buy, sell or have in possession, any species of duck for purposes of propagation; and *provided, further*, that a person, firm or corporation dealing in game or engaged in the cold storage business may have in possession for storage any species of duck between the first day of March and the first day of September following, if such birds were not taken or killed in this commonwealth contrary to the provisions of this chapter, or were not taken, killed, or transported contrary to the law of the state or country in which such birds were taken or killed, and *provided*, that such persons, firms or corporations shall have notified in writing the commissioners on fisheries and game on or before March first of the species, number of each species, and place of storage of such birds, and that such birds are in places and packages convenient for sealing.   The commissioners or their deputies shall then place a seal upon all receptacles and packages containing any species of wild duck.   The said seal shall not be removed by any person other than the commissioners on fisheries and game, or their deputies, under a penalty of twenty dollars for each bird,

and shall be removed by the said commissioners
or their deputies upon the first day of September
of each year.   The packages or contents thereof
so sealed shall not be removed from that storage
warehouse under a penalty of twenty dollars for
each bird.

SECTION 2.   Section four of chapter ninety-
two of the Revised Laws is hereby repealed.

SECTION 3.   Whoever violates any provision
of this act shall be punished by a fine of twenty
dollars for each bird or part thereof, in respect
to which the violation occurs.

SECTION 4.   This act shall take effect on the
first day of January in the year nineteen hundred
and seven.

ACTS OF 1905, CHAP. 273.

Shooting wild ducks and geese in Dukes county.

SECTION 1.   It shall be unlawful in the county
of Dukes County for any person to shoot or kill
wild ducks or geese in any fresh water pond from
a boat, raft or other device located at a greater
distance than fifty yards from the shore.

SECTION 2.   Any person violating any provision of this act shall be punished by a fine of
not less than five nor more than two hundred and
fifty dollars.

ACTS OF 1908, CHAP. 331.

**Pursuit and shooting of wild fowl in certain waters
of the town of Edgartown.**

SECTION 1.   No person shall, in or with any
boat, hunt, chase or pursue any wild water-fowl
in the inner harbor of Edgartown, including those
parts known as Katama bay and Mattakessett
bay, or in Cape Poge pond, so-called, in Edgartown, or in that part of the outer harbor of Edgartown which lies southerly or easterly of a
straight line drawn from Cape Poge lighthouse to
and through and onward from the harbor lighthouse of Edgartown; and no person shall in or
upon any of said waters shoot at any wild water-

fowl from any boat unless said boat be lying at anchor or be stationed upon the shore or other land or upon or against the ice: *provided, however*, that for the purpose of killing and securing any wild water-fowl just wounded by him or his companion, in lawful shooting, any person may pursue such wounded fowl with a boat, propelled by oar or oars only, to a distance not exceeding one hundred yards from the spot where the same was wounded, and may shoot the same from said boat within said distance.

SECTION 2.   Whoever violates any provision of this act shall be punished by a fine of not less than five or more than fifty dollars.

ACTS OF 1907, CHAP. 264.

Hunting wild ducks or geese on fresh water ponds in the county of Dukes county.

SECTION 1.   It shall be unlawful in the county of Dukes County for any person to pursue, drive, hunt, injure, shoot or kill wild ducks or geese in any fresh water pond from a boat, raft or other floating device.

SECTION 2.   Any person violating any provision of this act shall be punished by a fine of not less than five nor more than two hundred and fifty dollars for each offence.

SECTION 3.   Any acts or parts of acts inconsistent herewith are hereby repealed.

ACTS OF 1906, CHAP. 292.

An act to prohibit the use of live duck decoys in the taking or killing of black ducks in the county of Nantucket.

SECTION 1.   It shall be unlawful to use live duck decoys for the taking or killing of black ducks in the county of Nantucket.

SECTION 2.   Whoever violates any provision of this act shall be punished by a fine of not less than twenty nor more than fifty dollars for each offence.

As AMENDED BY ACTS OF 1905, CHAP. 414.

Shore, marsh and beach birds, upland plover, wild pigeons, gulls and terns.

SECTION 5. Whoever takes or kills a plover, snipe, sandpiper, rail or any of the so-called shore, marsh or beach birds between the first day of March and the fifteenth day of July, a Bartramian sandpiper, also called upland plover, before the fifteenth day of July in the year nineteen hundred and ten, a wild or passenger pigeon, a Carolina or mourning dove, a gull or tern at any time, shall be punished by a fine of ten dollars for every bird so taken or killed.

CERTAIN BIRDS SHALL NOT BE KILLED, CAPTURED, ETC., OR EGGS OR NEST DISTURBED.

ACTS OF 1903, CHAP. 244.

Protection of certain marsh birds.

SECTION 1. Whoever takes or kills any heron or bittern, or has in possession any such bird or part thereof, whenever or wherever taken, shall be punished by a fine not exceeding ten dollars for every bird so taken or killed, or bird or part of a bird so had in possession.

SECTION 2. Nothing in this act shall prevent the owner or keeper of any trout pond or trout hatchery from killing any heron or bittern engaged in the act of destroying fish; nor shall anything herein contained prevent the taking or possession of said birds by natural history associations, museums, or holders of certificates authorizing the collection of specimens for scientific purposes.

As AMENDED BY ACTS OF 1904, CHAP. 369.

Shore and marsh birds can be sold only during open season.

SECTION 6. Whoever buys, sells, exposes for sale, or has in possession any of the birds named

in and protected by section five or section seven
of this chapter, during the time within which the
taking or killing thereof is prohibited, whenever
or wherever such birds may have been taken or
killed, shall be punished by a fine of ten dollars
for each bird; but a person, firm or corporation
dealing in game or engaged in the cold storage
business may have in possession, for storage purposes only, the so-called shore, marsh and beach
birds during the time within which the taking or
killing of them is prohibited.

R. L., CHAP. 92, SECT. 7, AS AMENDED BY ACTS OF 1907,
CHAP. 250.

Relative to certain birds of prey.

SECTION 1.   Whoever takes or kills a wild or
undomesticated bird not named in sections two,
three, four and five, except English sparrows,
crow blackbirds, crows, jays, the following named
birds of prey, — sharp-shinned hawk, cooper's
hawk, goshawk, red-tailed hawk, red-shouldered
hawk, duck hawk, pigeon hawk, barred owl,
great horned owl and snowy owl, — wild geese
and fresh water and sea fowl not named in
said sections, or wilfully destroys, disturbs or
takes a nest or eggs of any wild or undomesticated birds, except such as are not protected by
the provisions of this section, shall be punished
by a fine of ten dollars for each bird taken or
killed or each nest or egg destroyed, disturbed or
taken contrary to the provisions of this section;
but a person over twenty-one years of age, who
has a certificate from the commissioners on
fisheries and game or from the president of the
Boston Society of Natural History that he is
engaged in the scientific study of ornithology or
is collecting in the interest of a scientific in-
stitution, may at any season take or kill or take
the nests and eggs of an undomesticated bird,
except woodcock, ruffed grouse and quail; but
the provisions of this section shall not authorize

a person to enter upon private grounds without the consent of the owner thereof for the purpose of taking nests or eggs or killing birds. Said commissioners or the president of said society may at any time revoke such certificate.

SECTION 2. Section one of chapter one hundred and twenty-seven of the acts of the year nineteen hundred and two is hereby amended by striking out the words "birds of prey", in the fifth line, and inserting in place thereof the words: — the following named birds of prey, — sharp-shinned hawk, cooper's hawk, goshawk, red-tailed hawk, red-shouldered hawk, duck hawk, pigeon hawk, barred owl, great horned owl and snowy owl, — so as to read as follows: — *Section 1.* Whoever captures or has in possession a wild or undomesticated bird not named in sections two, three, four or five of chapter ninety-two of the Revised Laws, except English sparrows, crow blackbirds, crows, jays, the following named birds of prey, — sharp-shinned hawk, cooper's hawk, goshawk, red-tailed hawk, red-shouldered hawk, duck hawk, pigeon hawk, barred owl, great horned owl and snowy owl, — wild geese and fresh water and sea fowl not named in said sections, and birds which are not found wild within the Commonwealth of Massachusetts, shall be punished by a fine of ten dollars, but this act shall not apply to birds held in captivity before this act takes effect.

ACTS OF 1903, CHAP. 329.

Bodies or feathers of certain birds.

SECTION 1. Whoever has in possession the body or feathers of a bird, the taking or killing of which is prohibited by the provisions of the preceding section or of section five of this chapter whether taken in this commonwealth or elsewhere, or wears such feathers for the purpose of dress or ornament, shall be punished by a fine of ten dollars; but the provisions of this section shall not prohibit the taking or killing of such birds by the holders of certificates provided for in the preceding section, nor shall they apply to natural history associations or to the proprietors of museums, or other collections for scientific purposes, or to non-residents of the commonwealth passing through it or temporarily dwelling therein.

SECTION 2.   This act shall take effect on the first day of January in the year nineteen hundred and four.

ACTS OF 1907, CHAP. 161.

The special game laws in Bristol county made uniform with the General Laws.

Chapter three hundred and sixty-six of the acts of the year nineteen hundred and four is hereby repealed.

ACTS OF 1908, CHAP. 284.

Close season on gray squirrels.

SECTION 1.   It shall be unlawful before the first day of October in the year nineteen hundred and ten to hunt, take or kill a gray squirrel, or to sell, or to offer for sale, or to have in possession for the purpose of sale, a gray squirrel taken or killed in Massachusetts.

SECTION 2.   This act shall not apply to the owner or occupant of any dwelling house or other building, who shall find any gray squirrel or squirrels doing damage to the same.

SECTION 3.   All acts and parts of acts inconsistent herewith are hereby repealed.

SECTION 4.   Whoever violates any provision of this act shall forfeit ten dollars for each offence.

AS AMENDED BY ACTS OF 1907, CHAP. 166.

Squirrels, hares and rabbits (compare preceding section which repeals provisions of this section relative to squirrels).

SECTION 9.   Whoever takes or kills a gray squirrel, between the first day of December and the first day of October, or a hare or rabbit be-

tween the first day of March and the first day
of October, or within said time, buys, sells or
offers for sale any of said animals, shall be punished by a fine of ten dollars; but any person,
firm or corporation dealing in game or engaged
in the cold storage business may buy, sell or have
in possession, and any person may buy from such
person, firm or corporation, and have in possession if so bought, Colorado jack rabbits, Nova
Scotia white or eastern white rabbits at any
season if they have not been taken or killed in
this commonwealth contrary to the provisions of
this section.

ACTS OF 1908, Chap. 413.

Sale of hares and rabbits legally killed.

SECTION 1. It shall be lawful at any time for
any person, firm or corporation engaged in the
cold storage business to buy or sell hares or
rabbits which have not been taken or killed contrary to the laws of this commonwealth or of any
other state or country.

SECTION 2. All acts and parts of acts inconsistent herewith are hereby repealed.

AS AMENDED BY ACTS OF 1906, CHAP. 241.

Use of traps, snares, ferrets, etc., illegal.

SECTION 11. Whoever takes or kills a game
bird or water fowl, hare or rabbit by means of a
trap, net or snare, or by the use of a ferret; and
whoever, for the purpose of taking or killing a
game bird, water fowl, hare or rabbit, constructs
or sets a trap, snare or net or uses a ferret; and
whoever shoots at or kills any wild fowl or any
of the so-called shore, marsh or beach birds with
a swivel or pivot gun or by the use of a torch,
jack or artificial light, or pursues any wild fowl
with or by the aid of a boat propelled by steam
or naphtha, or of a boat or vessel propelled by any
mechanical means other than sails, oars or pad-
dles, or in that portion of Boston harbor lying
westerly and southwesterly of a line running
from Deer Island to Point Allerton, including the

waters of Dorchester bay, Quincy bay, Weymouth bay and Hingham bay, shoots at, kills or pursues a wild fowl from or by the aid or use of any boat or floating device propelled by steam, naphtha, gasoline, electricity, compressed air, or any similar motive power, shall be punished by a fine of twenty dollars for each offence. The constructing or setting of a trap, snare or net adapted for the taking or killing of a game bird, water fowl, hare or rabbit, upon premises frequented by them, shall be prima facie evidence of such constructing and setting with intent to take and kill contrary to law; and possession of a ferret in a place where the game mentioned in this section might be taken or killed, shall be prima facie evidence that the person having it in possession has used it for taking and killing game contrary to law. Ferrets which are used in violation of the provisions of this section shall be confiscated.

As AMENDED BY ACTS OF 1906, CHAP. 278.

Snaring on own land.

SECTION 12. The provisions of the preceding section shall not apply to the trapping, other than by snare, of hares or rabbits upon his land by an owner of land, or by a member of his family if authorized by him, between the first day of October and the first day of December.

Shooting, Plymouth bay.

SECTION 13. Whoever in Plymouth harbor or bay, so-called, including the waters adjacent to the towns of Plymouth, Kingston and Duxbury, shoots at, kills or pursues a black duck, goose, brant or other aquatic bird by the use of a sneak boat, raft, floating box or similar device, not an ordinary dory or rowboat, or by the use of a pivot gun or swivel gun or any other firearm not usually held and discharged from the shoulder shall be punished by a fine of not less than ten nor more than fifty dollars.

Trespass.

SECTION 14. Whoever, for the purpose of shooting or trapping, enters upon land without permission of the owner thereof, after such owner has conspicuously posted thereon notice that shooting or trapping thereon is prohibited, shall be punished by a fine of not more than twenty dollars.

Ownership of game.

SECTION 15. Game artificially propagated and maintained upon land, upon which notice has been posted as provided in the preceding section, shall be the exclusive property of the person propagating and maintaining it, but if he sells such game for food at seasons when its capture is prohibited by law, he shall be punished by a fine of not more than twenty dollars.

ACTS OF 1908, CHAP. 477.

Mongolian, Chinese, English and Golden pheasants.

SECTION 1. It shall be unlawful to hunt, pursue, take, kill or have in possession, except for purposes of propagation, a Mongolian, Chinese, Golden or English Pheasant.

SECTION 2. Upon application to the commissioners on fisheries and game, written permission may be granted by them to a land owner engaged in rearing pheasants to shoot pheasants on his own premises to a number not exceeding the number actually reared to maturity by him in the year in which such permission is granted.

SECTION 3. Any person violating the provisions of this act shall be punished by a fine not exceeding fifty dollars for each bird or part thereof in respect to which the violation occurs.

SECTION 4. Section sixteen of chapter ninety-two of the Revised Laws, as amended by chapter seventy-three of the acts of the year nineteen hundred and five, and chapter four hundred and eighty-two of the acts of the year nineteen hundred and six, are hereby repealed.

DEER.

R. L., CHAP. 92, SECT. 17, AS AMENDED BY ACTS OF 1907,
CHAP. 307, AS FURTHER AMENDED BY ACTS OF 1908,
CHAP. 377.

The protection of deer.

SECTION 17. Whoever before the first day of November in the year nineteen hundred and ten, hunts, chases, wounds or kills a deer, or sells or offers for sale, or has in his possession for the purpose of sale, a deer captured or killed in Massachusetts except his own tame deer kept on his own grounds, or except a deer killed under the provisions hereinafter set forth, shall forfeit one hundred dollars for each offence: *provided, however,* that nothing contained herein shall prevent a farmer or other person, or any member of his family or person employed by him acting under his direction, from chasing, wounding or killing by use of a shotgun, any deer which he can prove was found injuring or destroying any crop or fruit tree upon the cultivated land owned or occupied by him. Any farmer or other person killing a deer found injuring or destroying any crop or fruit tree, or causing any deer to be killed by any member of his family or person employed by him as aforesaid shall forfeit the sum of one hundred dollars, unless he shall in writing under his signature report such killing forthwith to the clerk of the city or town in which the deer was killed, and shall upon the same day on which said deer was killed deliver to the clerk aforesaid the carcass of the deer so killed, which shall be sold by said clerk and the proceeds of said sale forwarded to the commissioners on fisheries and game for the uses of the said commissioners. The said report shall state the time and place of the killing, and the crop or tree which was being injured or destroyed by the deer, and shall be recorded by the clerk receiving it, who shall thereupon forward it to said commissioners.

As amended by Acts of 1905, Chap. 245.

Protection of deer from dogs.

Section 18. The owner or keeper of a dog found chasing or hunting deer at any time may be punished by a fine of not more than twenty dollars. Any of the commissioners on fisheries and game, or their deputies, or any member of the district police, or any officer qualified to serve criminal process, may kill a dog found chasing or hunting deer at any time if the dog is used for such purpose with the knowledge and consent of such owner or keeper, and the owner or keeper of such dog shall be punished by a fine of fifty dollars. If a dog has twice been found chasing or hunting deer, and if the owner or keeper of the dog has so been notified on each occasion by the commissioners on fisheries and game, it shall be a presumption of law, if the same dog is thereafter found chasing or hunting deer, that such chasing or hunting was with the knowledge and consent of the said owner or keeper, unless the contrary is shown by evidence.

Acts of 1903, Chap. 407.

Recovery for damages caused by wild deer.

Whoever suffers loss by the eating, browsing or trampling of his fruit or ornamental trees, vegetables, produce or crops by wild deer may, if the damage is done in a city, inform the officer of police of said city, who shall be designated to receive such information by the mayor, and if the damage is done in a town, may inform the chairman of the selectmen of the town wherein the damage was done, who shall proceed to the premises where the damage was done and determine whether the same was inflicted by deer, and if so, appraise the amount thereof if it does not exceed twenty dollars. If, in the opinion of said officer of police or chairman, the amount of said damage exceeds twenty dollars, he shall appoint two dis-

interested persons, who, with himself, shall
appraise under oath the amount thereof. The
said officer of police or chairman shall return a
certificate of the damages found, except in the
county of Suffolk, to the treasurer of the county
in which the damage is done, within ten days after
such appraisal is made. The treasurer shall
thereupon submit the same to the county commissioners, who, within thirty days, shall examine all such bills, and if any doubt exists, may
summon the appraisers and all parties interested
and make such examination as they may think
proper, and he shall transmit such bills, properly
approved, to the auditor of accounts, and they
shall be paid out of the treasury of the commonwealth in the same manner as other claims against
the commonwealth. In the county of Suffolk
the certificate of damages shall be returned to
the treasurer of the city or town in which the
damage is done, who shall exercise and perform
the rights and duties hereby conferred and imposed upon the county commissioners in other
counties. The appraisers shall receive from the
county, — or in the county of Suffolk, from the
city or town treasurer — one dollar each for every
such examination made by them, and the officer
or the chairman of selectmen acting in the case
shall receive twenty cents a mile, one way, for his
necessary travel.

Authority of commissioners.

SECTION 19. The authority of the commissioners on fisheries and game and of their deputies
shall extend to the propagation, protection and
preservation of birds and animals in like manner
as to fish.

As AMENDED BY ACTS OF 1907, CHAP. 300.

Disposal of fines.

SECTION 20. (Repealed March 31, 1908; compare Acts of 1908, chap. 330, p. 65.)

Game not to be transported out of state.

SECTION 21. Whoever at any time takes or sends or causes to be taken or transported beyond the limits of the commonwealth a woodcock, quail or ruffed grouse, which has been taken or killed within the commonwealth, or has in possession such bird or birds with intent to take or cause the same to be taken out of the commonwealth, shall be punished by a fine of ten dollars for every bird so had in possession or taken or caused to be taken or sent beyond the limits of the commonwealth as aforesaid.

ACTS OF 1902, CHAP. 236.

SECTION 1. Whoever, except as provided in section twenty-one of chapter ninety-two of the Revised Laws, takes or sends or causes to be taken or sent out of the commonwealth any bird or animal protected by the provisions of said chapter which has illegally been taken or killed within the commonwealth; and whoever has in possession any such bird or animal with intent to take or send the same or to cause the same to be taken or sent out of the commonwealth, shall be punished by a fine of twenty dollars for every bird or animal so had in possession or taken or sent beyond the limits of the commonwealth.

SECTION 2. Section twenty-two of chapter ninety-two of the Revised Laws is hereby repealed.

Introduction of foxes or raccoons into Dukes county prohibited.

SECTION 23. Whoever knowingly introduces into the county of Dukes County and liberates therein a fox or raccoon shall be punished for each offence by a fine of not less than twenty-five nor more than fifty dollars or by imprisonment for not more than thirty days, or by both such fine and imprisonment. The county commissioners of said county may offer a reward for the destruction of hawks, foxes and raccoons, and authorize the payment thereof by the county upon proper proof of such destruction.

English sparrows to be killed.

SECTION 24. The officers having charge of public buildings in cities and such officers as the selectmen designate and appoint in towns shall take and enforce such reasonable means and use such appliances, except poison, as in their judgment will effectively exterminate the English sparrow in such city or town. Whoever wilfully resists such officers while engaged in such duties or knowingly interferes with the means used by them for such purpose so as to render them less effective shall be punished by a fine of not more than twenty-five dollars for each offence. The provisions of this section shall not authorize an officer to enter on private property without the consent of the owner or occupant thereof.

ACTS OF 1903, CHAP. 344.

A bounty for killing a wild cat, Canada lynx or loupcervier.

SECTION 1. Whoever in any town kills a wild cat, Canada lynx or loupcervier not being in captivity shall, upon producing satisfactory evidence of such killing, be entitled to receive from the treasurer of the town the sum of five dollars; and all sums so paid out shall be repaid to the town treasurer by the treasurer of the county in which the town is situated: *provided*, that a sworn statement thereof shall be transmitted by the town treasurer to the county treasurer.

LIST OF PONDS STOCKED.

LIST OF PONDS STOCKED IN ACCORDANCE WITH SECTION 19, CHAPTER 91, REVISED LAWS, AS AMENDED BY ACTS OF 1903, CHAPTER 274, WITH REGULATIONS APPLIED THERETO.

[NOTE. — The following regulations apply to these ponds for a period of three years, beginning Nov. 1, 1906: The ponds are closed to all fishing from November 1 to May 30 of each year. Fishing with a hand line and single hook, or with a single hook and line attached to a rod or pole held in the hand, is permitted every day except Sunday in the ponds from May 30 to November 1, and in its tributary streams from April 15 to November 1.]

Ponds stocked in 1905.

Onota Lake . . .	Pittsfield . .	Closed until Dec. 1, 1908
Foster's . . .	Andover . .	Closed until Dec. 1, 1908
Dennison Lake . .	Winchendon .	Closed until Dec. 1, 1908
Naukeag Lake . .	Ashburnham .	Closed until Dec. 1, 1908
Crystal Lake . .	Gardner . .	Closed until Dec. 1, 1908
Nabnasset . . .	Westford . .	Closed until Dec. 1, 1908
Whalom 'Lake . .	Lunenburg .	Closed until Dec. 1, 1908
Round . . .	Tewksbury .	Closed until Dec. 1, 1908
Garfield Lake . .	Monterey . .	Closed until Dec. 1, 1908
Walden Lake . .	Concord . .	Closed until Dec. 1, 1908

Ponds stocked in 1905 — concluded.

Peter's	. . . . .	Dracut . . .	Closed until Dec. 1, 1908
Nagog	. . . . .	Acton and Littleton	Closed until Dec. 1, 1908
Robbin's	. . . . .	East Bridgewater	Closed until Dec. 1, 1908
Cooper's	. . . . .	North Carver .	Closed until Dec. 1, 1908
Whitman's	. . . . .	Weymouth	Closed until Dec. 1, 1908
Lead Mine	. . . . .	Sturbridge	Closed until Dec. 1, 1908
Big Alum	. . . . .	Sturbridge	Closed until Dec. 1, 1908
Winnecunnett	. . . . .	Norton .	Closed until Dec. 1, 1908
Great Pond	. . . . .	North Andover	Closed until Dec. 1, 1908

Ponds stocked in 1906.

Crane	. . . . .	West Stockbridge	Closed until Nov. 1, 1909
Mud .	. . . . :	West Stockbridge	Closed until Nov. 1, 1909
Keyes	. . . . .	Westford .	Closed until Nov. 1, 1909
Forge	. . . . .	Westford	Closed until Nov. 1, 1909
Spectacle	. . . . .	Littleton and Ayer .	Closed until Nov. 1, 1909
Wachusett Lake	. . . . .	Princeton and Westminster	Closed until Nov. 1, 1909
Nutting's	. . . . .	Billerica	Closed until Nov. 1, 1909
Spectacle	. . . . .	Sandwich	Closed until Nov. 1, 1909
Dennis	. . . . .	Yarmouth	Closed until Nov 1, 1909

Bloody	Plymouth	Closed until Nov. 1, 1909
Fresh	Orleans	Closed until Nov. 1, 1909
Tispaquin	Middleborough	Closed until Nov. 1, 1909
Hampton	Westfield	Closed until Nov. 1, 1909
Congamond Lake	Southwick	Closed until Nov. 1, 1909
Benton	Otis	Closed until Nov. 1, 1909
Pratt	Upton	Closed until Nov. 1, 1909
Attitash Lake	Amesbury	Closed until Nov. 1, 1909
Archer's	Wrentham	Closed until Nov. 1, 1909
Pearl Lake	Wrentham	Closed until Nov. 1, 1909
Moore's	Warwick	Closed until Nov. 1, 1909
Hardwick	Hardwick	Closed until Nov. 1, 1909
Pottapaug	Dana	Closed until Nov. 1, 1909
Flax	Lynn	Closed until Nov. 1, 1909
Little Alum	Brimfield	Closed until Nov. 1, 1909
Winthrop Lake	Holliston	Closed until Nov. 1, 1909

Ponds stocked in 1907.

Stiles Pond	Boxford	Closed until Dec. 1, 1910
Little Chauncy Pond	Northborough	Closed until Dec. 1, 1910
Pleasant Lake	Harwich	Closed until Dec. 1, 1910
Queen Lake	Phillipston	Closed until Dec. 1, 1910

Ponds stocked in 1907 — concluded.

Massapoag Lake	Sharon	Closed until Dec. 1, 1910
Monponsett Pond	Halifax	Closed until Dec. 1, 1910
Quannapowitt Lake	Wakefield	Closed until Dec. 1, 1910
Goose Pond	Chatham	Closed until Dec. 1, 1910
Scargo Lake	Dennis	Closed until Dec. 1, 1910
Prospect Pond	Taunton	Closed until Dec. 1, 1910
Long Pond	Royalston	Closed until Dec. 1, 1910
Horse Pond	Yarmouth	Closed until Dec. 1, 1910
Greenough Pond	Yarmouth	Closed until Dec. 1, 1910
Great Herring Pond	Plymouth	Closed until Dec. 1, 1910
Little Herring Pond	Plymouth	Closed until Dec. 1, 1910
Baddacook Pond	Groton	Closed until Dec. 1, 1910

GAME—WHEN TO BE KILLED.

		PENALTIES.
PARTRIDGE, WOODCOCK and QUAIL	between Nov. 1 and Oct. 1	$20
WOOD DUCK	not to be killed at any time	$20
BLACK DUCK or TEAL	between March 1 and Sept. 1	$20
ALL other kinds of DUCKS	between May 20 and Sept. 1	$20
LOONS	not to be hunted or killed in fresh water	$20
HARES and RABBITS	between March 1 and Oct. 1	$10
GRAY SQUIRRELS	are not to be killed at any time	$10
DEER	unless doing damage to buildings	$100
	are not to be killed at any time	$20–$50
Not to be chased with dogs.		
Damages by deer to be reimbursed.		
TRAPPING, SNARING and FERRETING of BIRDS and ANIMALS, and SETTING SNARES	prohibited	$20
MONGOLIAN, ENGLISH and GOLDEN PHEASANTS	are not to be killed at any time	$20

Game—when not to be killed—concluded.

INSECTIVOROUS and SONG BIRDS, EAGLES, FISH HAWKS, MARSH HAWKS and small OWLS, UPLAND PLOVER, WILD PIGEONS, HERONS, BITTERN, all GULLS and TERNS .	are not to be killed, captured, or held in possession at any time .	$10
PLOVER, SNIPE, RAIL and MARSH or BEACH BIRDS, .	between March 1 and July 15 .	$10
SALE of PARTRIDGE, PRAIRIE CHICKENS and WOODCOCK .	prohibited .	$20
SALE of QUAIL, killed in the State .	prohibited .	$20
SALE of SHORE, MARSH and BEACH BIRDS .	prohibited except during open season, for each bird .	$10
SENDING or carrying game out of the State .	prohibited .	$20
HUNTING on the Lord's Day .	prohibited .	$10–$20
KILLING or POSSESSION of PINNATED GROUSE (HEATH HEN) .	prohibited .	$100

NOTE. — The commissioners request that, in cold, stormy weather, or when the ground is covered with deep snow, citizens will feed the wild birds as opportunity comes to them. The sweepings of barn floors or refuse from tables will do much to relieve suffering and preserve life. Pieces of meat or fat hung to branches of trees will be eaten by birds.

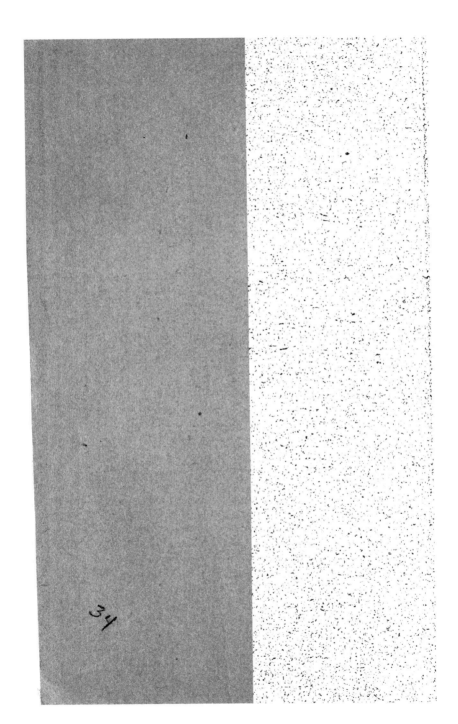

34